Gluten-Free
Cooking Made Easy

Gluten-Free
Cooking Made Easy
delicious recipes for everyone

Susan Bell

The publisher and the author of this cookbook are not responsible for health concerns that require medical supervision. Every effort has been made to provide the latest information on the gluten-free products called for in these recipes. Labels on products must be read to ensure that gluten has not been added since the publication of this book. The author assumes no responsibility for errors or changes that occur after publication.

Walnut Springs Press, LLC
110 South 800 West
Brigham City, Utah 84302
http://walnutspringspress.blogspot.com

ISBN: 978-1-935217-86-2

This book is an expanded version of *Gluten-free: Favorite Homestyle Recipes and Cooking Tips* (Susan Bell, 2008).

Table of Contents

Acknowledgements

I would like to thank my mother, Carol George, and my sisters, Mary Beth Wright and Cyndi Wakefield, who have contributed delicious recipes and who helped immensely with the book. And I will always be grateful to my husband, who has expanded my vision toward a greater summit.

Foreword

Author's Note: Peter HR Green, M.D., is one of the most well-known representatives and advocates for those of us with celiac disease. His important book, Celiac Disease: A Hidden Epidemic, *is written in a clear and helpful manner. In the book, he addresses the many symptoms of celiac disease, including digestive and neurological conditions. At the Celiac Disease Center at Columbia University, Dr. Green and his team do groundbreaking work to help people struggling with the disease. Dr. Green has appeared on various television shows, including* Good Morning America.

People with celiac disease and gluten sensitivity need to own a copy of this book. It is a great resource presented in a beautiful way. The recipes add diversity and nutrition to a diet that frequently lacks these important components.

Celiac disease is common, occurring in about 1% of the population worldwide. It is unfortunate that the majority of those who have the disease are yet to be diagnosed. There is a lack of physician awareness about the disease, its frequency, its great variety of manifestations, and its ease of diagnosis. As a result the majority of those with the disease are unaware of how their life could be altered for the better by adopting a gluten-free lifestyle.

Because of underdiagnosis, those with the disease lack adequate support systems. There is insufficient food labeling, lack of awareness in the food industry, inadequate knowledge among chefs, and a generally inadequate availability of gluten-free products. When products are available they are usually more expensive than gluten-containing products. School, college, and eating out of the home are a minefield. Susan's book helps fill the void. It is readily readable, and the food looks great!

People with gluten sensitivity experience symptoms that are relieved by avoiding gluten, which is found in wheat, rye, and barley. These people are often self-diagnosed. Diagnosing celiac disease typically requires a small-intestinal biopsy and documented improvement, both clinical and pathological. Blood tests often suggest the diagnosis; a small-intestinal biopsy confirms it. We encourage a biopsy because one needs to be certain of the diagnosis prior to making a lifelong commitment to a gluten-free diet. This especially applies to children.

We at the Celiac Disease Center at Columbia University are attempting to fill the medical void by increasing the quality of the patient care of those with celiac disease, educating health-care professionals, and facilitating a great variety of research projects. It is through dietician, nutritionist, and physician education that more will be diagnosed with celiac disease and their care will improve. Until the number of people diagnosed with celiac disease increases, the difficulties will continue. However, wonderful cookbooks like this one can lessen the burden of the disease.

Peter HR Green, M.D.
Author of *Celiac Disease: A Hidden Epidemic*
Professor of Clinical Medicine
The Celiac Disease Center
Columbia University, New York

Introduction

I started having stomach problems when I was eighteen, and for ten years I was misdiagnosed. I was diagnosed with irritable bowel syndrome (IBS), lactose intolerance, and anxiety. I also started having other health problems. I developed a goiter and became hypothyroid. I was also anemic and amenorrheaic. Then I developed stress fractures and found out I was osteopenic, even though I grew up drinking three glasses of milk a day. My symptoms increased to the point where I was spending half the day in the bathroom. I could not eat within six hours of running or else I was in the bathroom every thirty minutes. I finally told my doctors I could not live like this. After looking over my ten-year medical history, they decided I had celiac disease.

At first, I did not believe them. How could a wheat and gluten allergy cause all those symptoms? However, after three weeks on a gluten-free diet, I was spending much less time in the bathroom, I was not bloating after every meal, and my stomach did not hurt as much. At first, it was difficult to stay on the diet, and I ate a lot of chocolate. Six months later, I was able to tolerate milk again. At that point, I ate a lot of ice cream. I slowly started to find gluten-free alternatives. I missed a lot of foods, but not the way they made me feel.

Now, three years later, I can see and feel the difference in my body. I am no longer anemic or amenorrheaic. Plus, I accomplished a lifelong dream of making the U.S. Olympic team in the 10,000 meters. I competed in Beijing, representing the USA and placing 26th. I would not have been able to accomplish this goal had I not gotten that celiac disease diagnosis.

For some people the celiac diagnosis is a prison sentence, but I was set free by it. I no longer had pain, and I didn't have to plan my day and my training runs around bathroom locations. Giving up pasta, wheat, and gluten can seem like a huge sacrifice, but the returns are worth it. I gave up wheat and gluten, but in return I regained my health and the Olympic dream.

Giving up wheat and gluten does not mean giving up your favorite foods. There are so many new gluten-free alternatives to try. There are also great people who have taken the time to turn old favorite recipes into gluten-free ones. This cookbook is a good place to start. Susan Bell has taken many of the best comfort foods and made them gluten free. She has also filled this book with tips and advice on cooking and eating gluten free. If you feel deprived of your favorite comfort meal, just open the pages of this book and get started on gluten-free cooking.

Amy Yoder Begley, celiac Olympian

Useful Information

The Scoop about Gluten-Free Cooking

When I asked my eleven-year-old daughter what others should know about gluten-free cooking, she said, "Don't forget the xanthan gum!" She knows that we have had several failures when we have tried to bake bread, muffins, or cookies without xanthan gum. These baked good simply won't hold together without it. We tend to forget the xanthan gum most often when we are trying to convert a wheat-flour recipe to a gluten-free recipe.

One of the first disappointments I experienced with gluten-free cooking was the change in the texture and look of baked bread and rolls. Gluten-free bread and rolls are denser, misshapen, and a bit grainy. Before I got celiac disease, my baking included white bread and rolls that were light and fluffy. Once you get accustomed to the idea that it will never be the same, you can be happy with the success of baking anything that is similar in taste to wheat-based items.

When it comes to baking gluten-free bread, I didn't have any success without the use of smaller bread pans. If you use regular-sized bread pans, you might as well bring in a brick and place it on the table, because the bread will be very similar!

We seldom bought corn tortillas previous to going on a gluten-free diet, unless we were making enchiladas. Now we use corn tortillas nearly every day. Corn tortillas taste terrible, in my opinion, in their original state. We fry them, microwave them in a cloth packet or between moist paper towels, and bake them. One of our favorite after-school snacks is Pizza Tortillas (see recipe with Tortilla Wrap Ideas). When our children have their friends come over to play, they often request this snack.

In this book, I have tried to include clear directions on how to make homestyle recipes like gravy and roast beef. We can't always call home and ask our mother how to do it, so it is nice to have directions on how to cook certain items. In the past, we made gravy with white flour. We have found that we can make delicious gravy with cornstarch. Just remember to combine cornstarch with a liquid that is not hot; otherwise, there will be plenty of lumps.

With my cookbook, you can feed your entire family with delicious recipes that are gluten free. There is no need to have two menus for dinner. Recipes for some of the foods you miss the most are included in the cookbook, such as pizza, ice cream cones, and bread. These recipes will definitely satisfy people who are used to eating foods made from wheat.

Kitchen Basics

To cook and bake gluten-free, you will need to keep several ingredients on hand, some of which are rather expensive. The first time I tried making gluten-free bread, I was shocked at the cost of all of the ingredients. I had no idea xanthan gum was nearly as valuable as gold! The number of grains the recipe called for was a bit surprising; in fact, the ingredients for one loaf of bread covered more than half of my counter space. In addition to the xanthan gum, I found I needed to buy brown rice flour (now I grind it fresh), tapioca flour, potato starch, sorghum flour, corn flour, teff flour, quinoa flakes, etc., depending on which type of bread I wanted to make.

Here are a few tips to help make gluten-free cooking as simple as possible.

- Set up a "baking center" in your pantry. Store your flours and other dry ingredients in a row of plastic containers with snap-tight lids.
- Save money by buying larger bags of tapioca flour and potato starch. Keep a sifter in your potato starch container; get rid of the hard lumps before they end up in your muffins or cookies.
- Buy a good mixer. I use a Bosch, and it is wonderful for mixing gluten-free dough. There are other good brands of kitchen mixers available, such as Kitchen Aid.
- If someone in your household bakes with gluten, avoid being near the airborne flour dust. Have separate appliances for gluten-free cooking and regular cooking, to avoid cross-contaminating your gluten-free food.
- Buy several small bread pans. I like 8½ x 4½ x 2¾ inch.

- Buy two or three good muffin tins so you can make muffins in large batches and then freeze them.
- Use a mill to grind brown rice into flour. Mine is a K-TEC Kitchen Mill™ (K-TEC is now Blendtec). Since rice flour has a short shelf life, grinding your own will save you money.
- Consider purchasing an electric rice cooker. Typically, a gluten-free diet includes quite a bit of rice, so this will come in handy. You can also use the rice cooker for preparing gluten-free hot cereal. This especially works well with some gluten-free oatmeal, such as old-fashioned oats that can be hard to chew. Just pour in the hot cereal and water, turn the rice cooker to WARM for 15 minutes, and then switch it to COOK. When the moisture has absorbed (this usually takes 10 to 15 minutes), the rice cooker will automatically change back to the WARM setting, and the hot cereal is ready to serve.

With the right equipment and ingredients, gluten-free cooking can be much easier and more convenient than you ever imagined.

Eating Out

Those of us with celiac disease and wheat allergies are now full of hope that there will be something for us to eat at a restaurant besides a salad without croutons! Many restaurant owners have become aware of our disease and now provide gluten-free menus for our benefit.

When I was first diagnosed with celiac disease, I felt I couldn't eat out anymore because of the prevalence of wheat-based food. This mentality wasn't much fun, and I soon realized that I didn't want to miss out on the pleasure of eating out. I decided it was time to be proactive. I began calling restaurants (mid-afternoon, when they weren't quite as busy) and asking to speak with the cook to determine what foods I could eat. I told them how important it was that the grill they used to cook their steak or chicken breast wasn't cross-contaminated by another food with breading or seasonings and sauces that might have wheat. I explained that even the cooking oil for the French fries couldn't be the same oil used to fry things like breaded chicken.

My favorite Mexican restaurant fries their corn tortilla chips in the same oil as their flour tortillas. I was able to get permission from the manager to bring my own small bag of corn tortilla chips to the restaurant. I was then all set to dip my gluten-free chips into my own dish of their delicious gluten-free salsa. Sometimes we have to do things that are a little out of the ordinary to get the satisfaction and enjoyment we are searching for.

Many restaurant owners, managers, and cooks are understanding of food intolerance. We have a wonderful local restaurant that orders in gluten-free pizza crust so they can offer gluten-free pizza. They are careful to prepare and cook the gluten-free pizza in a separate part of the restaurant, away from airborne flour dust. Some cooks have been willing to fry my food in a separate skillet when the grill is cross-contaminated. It is amazing to see the level of support and kindness that many people show toward those of us dealing with a difficult diet.

Lessons and Warnings

Here are some lessons I have learned as a celiac, as well as some warnings I would like to pass along to you.

This information is subject to change, so make sure you read labels for the latest information.

- Some dried fruit may be coated with wheat flour to prevent the pieces from sticking together. Banana chips are often coated with flour.
- Medicine and vitamins may contain gluten. A good website to check is glutenfreedrugs.com.
- Deli roast beef (and other types of lunch meat) can contain wheat in the broth used to moisten the meat.
- Some prepared, flavored rice in packets (or served in restaurants) may contain wheat.
- Even though allergen warnings may say that a product doesn't contain wheat, it may contain gluten in the form of barley (malt), rye, or cross-contaminated oats. An example might be a candy bar containing crispy rice.

- Several people in our local support group have felt there is a connection between skin and scalp irritation and the wheat in lotions and hair products.
- It is important that restaurant employees understand the concept of cross-contamination on grills and in cooking oil. French fries cooked in the same oil as chicken nuggets are not considered gluten free. Many restaurants have gluten-free menus that are available online.
- Breath mints may contain wheat maltodextrin. Gum may contain wheat.\
- Coated nuts may contain wheat.
- Lipstick may contain wheat.
- Some potato chips now contain wheat flour or wheat maltodextrin. Maltodextrin, listed by itself, does not contain wheat or barley.
- Make sure you have your own peanut butter, jam, jelly, butter, honey, mayonnaise, etc. Labeling will help prevent cross-contamination.
- Corn tortillas and tostadas may have cross-contamination from flour tortillas produced in the same facility. Check the label. Wheat flour is used in the production of some corn tortillas to make the tortillas more firm. A fast-food establishment or restaurant should be able to refer to the labels on the boxes in which the tortillas were shipped, to give you this needed information.
- Be certain to read the label for these products: frosting, beef broth/bouillon, seasoning mix, gravy mix, hot dogs, salami, flavored tortilla chips, trail mix, artificial crab, marinades, and soy sauce.
- Purchased play dough often has wheat. For young children who tend to lick their fingers, it may be important to make homemade play dough (see pages 183 and 184).
- Buy an extra toaster to be used for gluten-free bread. Label it "For gluten-free bread only." Toaster ovens can also be used to toast bread, and the oven rack can be washed thoroughly and then used for toasting.
- Some people are so sensitive that touching gluten products or breathing white or wheat flour dust can affect them.
- Modified food starch produced in the U.S. is commonly made from corn. Also, caramel color, artificial flavors, and artificial colors are usually gluten free in this country.
- When children with celiac disease have gone to an event where they have been deprived of a treat, it may be helpful to have a supply of gluten-free

candy at home to give them when they arrive home. If possible, send the treat with them to the event.

- Serving gluten-free pizza from the health food store (or homemade pizza) can help ease the disappointment felt from missing out on pizza with gluten.
- Read labels! Companies are usually very helpful about providing information, and many phone numbers are toll free. When in doubt about a specific food item, call the manufacturer to verify that the food does not contain gluten.
- Gluten-free noodles, spaghetti sauce, rice, potato flakes, canned chicken, water, powdered milk, canned fruits, and canned vegetables are good to keep on hand for emergencies.
- When using emergency food storage, substitute canned chicken in place of fresh chicken in selected recipes that your family enjoys.
- Natural disasters are becoming more common. An emergency kit with a 72-hour supply of gluten-free food is a good idea.
- In uncertain economic times, it is important to have some food stored. Consider keeping extra gluten-free flour in the freezer for emergency use.
- Diagnosing celiac disease is still difficult for most of the medical profession. Most of the people in our support group were ill for an extended amount of time and consulted numerous doctors before discovering that they have gluten intolerance. The wide range of symptoms contributes to the difficulties of diagnosis.

There are many great foods to eat! With practice, you can enjoy a wonderful gluten-free lifestyle.

Meal Planning

Main-Dish Menu Ideas

Week 1
1. Baked Whole Chicken
2. Beef Stroganoff
3. Sweet and Sour Meatballs
4. Fried Fish and Irish Nachos
5. Tacos and Chili Relleno Casserole
6. Shrimp Stir-Fry
7. Easy Vegetable Noodle Casserole

Week 2
1. Roast Beef
2. Chinese Noodles
3. Baked Potato Bar
4. Chinese Sweet and Sour
5. Seasoned Pork Chops
6. Parmesan Cheese Chicken
7. Chicken Fettuccine

Week 3
1. Grilled Steak
2. Taco Salad and Quick Chicken Tortillas
3. Creamy Chicken Enchiladas
4. Hawaiian Haystacks
5. Bacon Ranch Hamburgers
6. Alfredo Pizza
7. Honey Mustard Chicken

Week 4
1. Steak Fajitas
2. Pineapple Chicken Lo Mein
3. Meatloaf
4. Spaghetti
5. Sausage Pizza
6. Hot and Spicy Chicken
7. Paprika Chicken

Week 5
1. Lemon Chicken
2. Shepherd's Pie
3. Grilled Salmon
4. Beef Enchiladas
5. Pizza
6. Thai Red Curry
7. Sweet and Sour Pork

Week 6
1. Sweet Pear Pork Chops
2. Japanese Style Chicken
3. Marinated Italian Halibut
4. Pork Roast
5. Green Chili Tacos
6. Barbecued Chicken
7. Chili Potato Topping

Week 7

1. Prize-winning Chili
2. Sweet and Sour Chicken
3. Chicken Strips
4. Salt and Vinegar Chicken
5. Slow-Cooked Roast
6. Tortilla Wraps (see Tortila Wrap Ideas in Main Dish section)
7. Chicken with Sweet Lemon Sauce

Week 8

1. Rich and Cheesy Halibut
2. Barbecued Meatballs
3. Ground Beef Gravy with Potatoes
4. Chicken Fajitas (see Steak Fajitas recipe)
5. Italian Chicken
6. Omelets or Mexican Sausage Bake
7. Honey Garlic Chicken

Week 9

1. Creamy Romano Chicken
2. Easy Quiche
3. Fish Tacos with Sweet Cucumber Salsa
4. Magnificent Steak Burritos
5. Parmesan Pork Chops
6. Red Sauce Creamy Enchiladas
7. Choose a Soup

Week 10

1. Barbequed Chicken with Smoked Sausage
2. Flavorful Baked Fish
3. Lemon Basil Chicken

4. Lasagna
5. Sweet and Sour Pork Ribs
6. Easy Chili
7. Tasty Sweet Pork Mexican Salad

Cold Weather Soups

Substitute in place of another menu item when desired.

Clam Chowder
Sausage Kale Soup
Thai Noodle Soup
Cream of Broccoli Soup
Enchilada Soup
Fiesta Soup
Baked Potato Soup
Chicken or Turkey Noodle Soup
Chicken Taco Soup
Beef Taco Soup
Turkey Burger Soup
Curried Chicken Rice Soup
Minestrone Soup
Cream of Rice Soup
Potato Bean Soup
Potato Cheese Soup
Best Cream of Tomato Soup
Broccoli Cheese Soup
Corn Chowder with Sweet Potatoes
Creamy Butternut Squash Soup
Egg Drop Soup
Fabulous Italian Sausage Soup
Russian Borscht
Savory Leek Soup
Sensational Tomato Basil Soup
White Bean and Chicken Soup

Breakfast

Best Waffles

3 eggs, separated

1¾ cups milk, almond milk,
   or soy milk

½ cup cooking oil

2 teaspoons vanilla

2 tablespoons melted butter

¾ cup brown rice flour

¼ cup sorghum flour

¼ cup potato starch

⅔ cup tapioca flour

⅛ cup corn flour

1 tablespoon plus 1 teaspoon
   baking powder

2 tablespoons sugar

½ teaspoon salt

⅓ cup butter

1. Heat waffle iron.

2. Separate the egg whites from the egg yolks.

3. Place egg whites in a glass bowl and beat until stiff.

4. In a separate mixing bowl, combine egg yolks, milk, cooking oil, vanilla, and melted butter. Mix well.

5. Add the dry ingredients and mix gently. Fold in egg whites.

6. Spray waffle iron with nonstick spray. Cook waffles according to waffle-iron directions.

Tip: To fold beaten egg whites into the batter, use a rubber spatula and make gentle circles in the batter while rotating your wrist.

Serves 5 to 7

Fluffy Oven Pancakes

6 eggs

1 cup milk, almond milk, or
   soy milk

1 teaspoon vanilla

¾ cup brown rice flour

¼ cup tapioca flour

½ teaspoon salt

1. Preheat oven to 400°F.

2. Melt butter in microwave and pour evenly into a 9 x 13-inch casserole dish.

3. In a large bowl, beat eggs, milk, and vanilla.

4. Add rice flour, tapioca flour, and salt. Mix with hand mixer until well combined.

5. Pour batter over melted butter. Bake for 22 to 24 minutes. Serve with powdered sugar and syrup.

Serves 4 to 6

Tip: Bake with the rack in the center of the oven to ensure that pancakes do not touch the top element of the oven when they puff up.

Favorite Pancakes

1 egg
½ cup applesauce
1½ cups milk
½ cup cooking oil
1 cup tapioca flour
⅓ cup sorghum flour
⅛ cup potato starch
⅛ cup corn flour
½ cup rice flour
1 tablespoon plus 1 teaspoon
*   baking powder*
1 tablespoon plus 1 teaspoon
*   sugar*
½ teaspoon salt

1. Preheat griddle.
2. Blend together egg, applesauce, milk and cooking oil. Add dry ingredients. Stir until moistened.
3. Fry pancakes on nonstick griddle until golden brown on each side. Serve with syrup.

Serves 6 to 8

Tip: Brown rice flour is higher in nutrient value than white rice flour, but because of the oils in the bran, it has a shorter shelf life and should be stored in a tight container in the fridge or freezer.

Caramel Syrup

½ cup butter
½ cup milk
1 cup brown sugar
1 cup sugar

1. Melt butter in a medium saucepan.
2. Add milk, brown sugar, and sugar. Stir and boil gently for one minute. Remove pan from stove and add buttermilk and vanilla.

Dairy-Free Syrup

1 cup water
¾ cup sugar
1 cup brown sugar
1 cup corn syrup
⅛ teaspoon salt
1 teaspoon vanilla
½ teaspoon butter flavoring

1. Bring water, sugar, brown sugar, corn syrup, salt, vanilla, and butter flavoring to a boil in a medium saucepan and reduce heat to medium-high.

2. Simmer for 1 minute.

Sausage Pizza

Crust

2 tablespoons butter
½ cup cornstarch
½ cup tapioca flour
¼ cup potato flour
1 teaspoon sugar
½ teaspoon salt
1 teaspoon baking powder
1 egg
¾ cup milk

1. Preheat oven to 400°F.

2. In a large bowl, blend butter and dry ingredients with a pastry cutter (or mix in a heavy-duty kitchen mixer).

3. In a small bowl, beat the milk with the egg. Pour milk and egg into mixture of dry ingredients and butter. Mix well.

4. Place a clean sandwich bag on your hand and press dough onto a large, greased pizza pan.

5. Bake crust for 10 minutes. Remove from oven and add topping.

Topping

10 sausage links
2 tablespoons brown rice
   flour

1. Cook sausage until browned and until middle is no longer pink.*

2. Remove sausage to a plate, leaving 2 tablespoons fat and drippings in pan.

3. Add rice flour to pan and blend well.

1½ cups milk
½ teaspoon gluten-free
chicken bouillon
4 eggs, with salt added
1 cup grated cheese

4. Stir in milk and chicken bouillon, then bring to a boil. Cook gravy until thickened, stirring constantly. Spread gravy over the pizza crust.

5. Cut sausage links into small chunks and spread on top of gravy.

6. Scramble eggs and sprinkle over the gravy and sausage.

7. Spread grated cheese over all.

8. Bake for 10 to 15 minutes. This pizza tastes best if allowed to sit for 5 to 10 minutes after baking.

Serves 8 to 10

*To prepare link sausages with a minimum amount of fat:

1. Place sausage in a frying pan and cover with a small amount of water.

2. Cover pan and cook sausage slowly for 5 to 10 minutes. Drain well.

3. With pan uncovered, continue to cook sausage slowly for 12 to 14 minutes until browned on all sides.

4. Cover sausage with a small amount of water and cook for three minutes on high heat. Cook the sausage longer, if needed, to ensure it is completely cooked.

Breakfast Burritos

1 tablespoon butter
3 green onions, chopped
½ green pepper, finely
    chopped
1 teaspoon crushed garlic
½ bag gluten-free hash
    browns, country style
2 to 3 eggs
salt, pepper, and garlic salt,
    to taste
1 cup grated cheese
gluten-free corn tortillas
salsa

1. Melt butter in skillet.
2. Add green onions, green pepper, and crushed garlic. Sauté for 2 to 3 minutes.
3. Add hash browns and continue cooking until they are warm and cooked through.
4. Add eggs and continue to cook.
5. When eggs are done, add salt, pepper, and garlic salt to taste.
6. Add cheese and heat until melted.
7. Place a scoop of egg mixture in a warmed corn tortilla and top with salsa.

Serves 5 to 7

Omelets

3 eggs
1 tablespoon water or milk
3 mushrooms, sliced
¼ cup diced green pepper
⅛ cup bacon pieces
⅛ cup green chilies
⅛ cup chopped olives
¼ cup diced green onions
¼ cup grated cheese

1. Beat eggs with water or milk.
2. Pour into a greased omelet pan or nonstick frying pan.
3. Sprinkle other ingredients onto eggs.
4. If using an omelet pan, follow instructions. If using a frying pan, place the toppings on one-half of the egg mixture and cook on medium heat until eggs turn light brown on the bottom. Then flip the uncovered half onto the other half. Flip the entire omelet again to complete the cooking of the eggs.

Serves 1

Tip: If you want tender green peppers, soften by cooking them in a small amount of butter before starting the omelet.

Breakfast Pizza

Crust

*24-ounce package gluten-
    free hash browns, thawed*
1 egg, beaten
½ teaspoon salt
¼ teaspoon pepper

Egg Topping

7 eggs
½ cup milk
1 teaspoon crushed garlic
½ teaspoon salt
¼ teaspoon pepper
1 cup chopped ham
¼ cup sliced green onions
*¼ cup chopped green bell
    pepper*
1½ cups shredded cheese
garlic salt, to taste
salsa

1. Preheat oven to 400°F.
2. Coat a large pizza pan with cooking spray.
3. Combine crust ingredients and spread across pizza pan, using the back of a spoon.
4. Bake for 20 minutes.
5. To make the topping, whisk eggs, milk, garlic, salt, and pepper together. Spread over the potato crust.
6. Top with remaining ingredients.
7. Bake for 20 to 30 minutes, or until eggs are cooked. Serve with salsa.

Serves 8 to 10

Mexican Sausage Bake

4 white corn tortillas
1 can chopped green chilies
*   (optional)*
½ pound sausage, cooked
*   and drained*
1 cup Monterey Jack cheese
5 eggs
¼ cup milk
¼ teaspoon salt
¼ teaspoon garlic salt
¼ teaspoon onion salt
¼ teaspoon pepper
¼ teaspoon ground cumin
paprika
sour cream
salsa

This dish can be prepared a few hours ahead or the day before, if covered and refrigerated. Remove from refrigerator 30 minutes before baking.

1. Preheat oven to 350°F.

2. Beat eggs, milk, and seasonings.

3. Pour ⅓ of egg and milk mixture into a greased 8 x 8-inch baking dish.

4. Slice tortillas to fit the square baking dish. Then layer ½ of tortillas, chilies, sausage, and cheese in the baking dish.

5. Follow this layer with ⅓ of the egg and milk mixture.

6. Repeat layer of tortillas, chilies, sausage, and cheese.

7. Cover with remaining ⅓ of the egg and milk mixture.

8. Sprinkle with paprika and bake uncovered for 40 to 45 minutes.

9. Remove from oven and let stand for 10 minutes.

10. Serve with sour cream and salsa.

Serves 4 to 5

Granola

7 brown rice cakes, in bite-
    sized pieces*
½ cup slivered almonds
½ cup raw sunflower seeds
½ cup sweetened or
    unsweetened coconut
1 teaspoon cinnamon
3 tablespoons olive oil
½ cup 100% pure maple
    syrup

1. Preheat oven to 300°F.
2. Combine broken rice cakes, almonds, sunflower seeds, coconut, and cinnamon in a bag. Shake to distribute cinnamon evenly.
3. Add oil and syrup. Shake until coated.
4. Spray or grease cookie sheet.
5. Bake granola for 7 minutes. Stir.
6. Bake an additional 8 to 10 minutes, or until granola is lightly browned.

Serves 3 to 5

* Place the rice cakes in a gallon-size ziptop bag. Seal bag and gently press with a rolling pin to break cakes into bite-size pieces.

Fruit Smoothie

1 cup vanilla soy milk
1 cup ice cubes
1 cup sliced strawberries,
    raspberries, peaches, or
    mixed berries
¼ cup sugar
2 tablespoons powdered milk
1 teaspoon vanilla

Combine in a blender using high speed until the mixture is smooth.

Serves 2 to 4

Orange Cream Smoothie

4 cups vanilla soy milk
½ can orange juice
  concentrate
½ cup sugar
¼ cup powdered milk
2 tablespoons sugar
1 teaspoon vanilla
8 ice cubes

Combine in a large blender using high speed for 1 to 2 minutes until the mixture is smooth and sugar dissolves.

Serves 8 to 10

Breads and Muffins

Poppyseed Muffins

3 eggs
1⅛ cups cooking oil
1½ cups milk or soy milk
1½ teaspoons almond extract
1½ teaspoons butter-flavored
*   extract*
1½ teaspoons vanilla
2 cups sugar
2 cups brown rice flour
1 tablespoon corn flour
2½ tablespoons sorghum
*   flour*
1⅛ cups tapioca flour
⅓ cup potato starch, sifted
1 teaspoon salt
1½ teaspoons baking
*   powder*
1 teaspoon xanthan gum
1 tablespoon poppyseeds

1. Preheat oven to 400°F.

2. Beat eggs, oil, milk, almond extract, butter-flavored extract, and vanilla in a large mixing bowl.

3. Add sugar, brown rice flour, corn flour, sorghum flour, tapioca flour, potato starch, salt, baking powder, xanthan gum and poppyseeds to wet ingredients. Stir gently.

4. Using a rubber spatula, flatten the largest remaining lumps in the batter.

5. Spoon batter into greased muffin tins, about ¾ full. (Cupcake liners are helpful for these muffins, since they tend to stick to the muffin tins.) Bake for 20 to 25 minutes.

6. If desired, poke holes in the warm muffins with a toothpick and pour glaze over them.

7. For bread, divide batter into two greased 8½ x 4½ x 2¾-inch bread pans. Bake at 350°F for 1 hour or more.

Optional Glaze

¼ cup undiluted limeade or
*   orange juice concentrate*
1 cup powdered sugar
½ teaspoon almond extract
½ teaspoon butter-flavored
*   extract*
½ teaspoon vanilla

1. Bring juice concentrate and powdered sugar to a boil for 1 minute.

2. Remove from heat and add extracts and vanilla.

3. Drizzle over muffins or bread.

Makes 22 to 24 muffins or 2 loaves of bread

Orange Cranberry Muffins

1½ cups buttermilk
¼ cup cooking oil
1 egg
1 cup sugar
½ tablespoon vanilla
*1 large orange, peeled and
    quartered*
*½ cup sweetened dried
    cranberries*
¾ cup brown rice flour
⅔ cup tapioca flour
¼ cup potato starch
*3 tablespoons sorghum
    flour*
2 tablespoons corn flour
½ teaspoon salt
1 teaspoon baking soda
*½ tablespoon baking
    powder*
2 teaspoons xanthan gum
⅔ cup sugar (for glaze)
*⅛ cup orange juice
    (for glaze)*

1. Preheat oven to 350°F.

2. Purée buttermilk, oil, egg, sugar, orange, and vanilla in blender until smooth.

3. Add dried cranberries, brown rice flour, tapioca flour, potato starch, sorghum flour, corn flour, salt, baking soda, baking powder and xanthan gum and mix until combined.

4. Spoon batter into greased muffin tins, about ¾ full. Bake for 20 to 24 minutes.

5. To make glaze, bring ⅔ cup sugar and ⅛ cup orange juice to a boil until sugar dissolves. Spoon glaze over the top of each muffin.

Makes 16 to 18 muffins

31

Pumpkin Muffins

8 eggs

1¾ cups cooking oil

29-ounce can pumpkin

2 teaspoons cinnamon

1 teaspoon allspice

1 teaspoon nutmeg

2 cups brown rice flour

1½ cups tapioca flour

½ cup sorghum flour

¼ cup corn flour

½ cup potato starch

4 cups sugar

*1 tablespoon plus 1 teaspoon
    xanthan gum*

*1 tablespoon plus 1 teaspoon
    baking powder*

*1 tablespoon plus 1 teaspoon
    baking soda*

2 teaspoons salt

*12-ounce package milk
    chocolate chips (optional)*

This recipe is large enough to make both bread and muffins. The bread and muffins freeze well.

1. Combine eggs, oil, pumpkin, cinnamon, allspice, and nutmeg, mixing well.

2. Add brown rice flour, tapioca flour, sorghum flour, corn flour, potato starch, sugar, xanthan gum, baking powder, baking soda, salt, and chocolate chips. Mix only until combined.

3. To make bread, grease pans (8½ x 4½ x 2¾ inches) and bake at 350°F for 60 minutes.

4. To make muffins, spoon into greased muffin tins, about ¾ full. Bake for 26 minutes at 400°F.

Makes 24 muffins plus 2 small loaves of bread

Tip: The following pan sizes are recommended for gluten-free bread recipes (measurements refer to the inside of the pan at the top edge): 8½ × 4½ × 2⅝ inches or 7¼ × 3⅝ × 2¼ inches.

Applesauce Muffins

2 eggs

1½ cups milk, almond milk,
   or soy milk

1 cup applesauce

1 cup cooking oil

1¼ cups brown rice flour

½ cup sorghum flour

¼ cup corn flour

4 tablespoons cornstarch or
   potato starch

1 cup tapioca flour

2 teaspoons xanthan gum

1 cup brown sugar

½ cup sugar

1 tablespoon plus 1 teaspoon
   baking powder

1 teaspoon salt

1½ teaspoons cinnamon

These muffins freeze well.

1. Preheat oven to 400°F.

2. Beat eggs.

3. Mix in milk, applesauce, and oil.

4. Add brown rice flour, sorghum flour, corn flour, cornstarch, tapioca flour, xanthan gum, brown sugar, sugar, baking powder, salt, and cinnamon. Mix just until moistened.

5. Spoon batter into greased muffin tins, about ¾ full. Bake for 20 to 25 minutes.

6. For bread, divide batter into two greased 8½ x 4½ x 2¾-inch bread pans. Bake at 350°F for 1 hour.

Makes 24 muffins or 2 loaves of bread.

Fact: Breads and cookies that call for applesauce or mashed bananas are moist and the flavor of the fruit enhances the gluten-free flours. The fruit increases the nutritional value.

Blueberry Muffins

1½ cups buttermilk

⅓ cup cooking oil

1 egg

1¼ cups sugar

½ tablespoon vanilla

⅔ cup sweetened dried
    blueberries

¾ cup brown rice flour

⅔ cup tapioca flour

¼ cup potato starch

3 tablespoons sorghum flour

2 tablespoons corn flour

½ teaspoon salt

1 teaspoon baking soda

½ tablespoon baking
    powder

2 teaspoons xanthan gum

1. Preheat oven to 350°F.
2. Combine buttermilk, oil, egg, sugar, vanilla, and dried blueberries.
3. Add brown rice flour, tapioca flour, potato starch, sorghum flour, corn flour, salt, baking soda, baking powder, and xanthan gum. Mix until combined.
4. Spoon batter into greased muffin tins, about ¾ full.
5. Bake for 17 to 19 minutes.

Makes 14 to 16 muffins

Zucchini Muffins

3 eggs, beaten

1 cup cooking oil

2 cups sugar

1 tablespoon vanilla

2 cups brown rice flour

1 cup tapioca flour

4 tablespoons potato starch

These muffins freeze well.

1. Preheat oven to 400°F.
2. Combine eggs, oil, sugar, and vanilla in a large mixing bowl.
3. Add dry ingredients and zucchini. Mix until combined.

1 teaspoon salt
1 tablespoon xanthan gum
1 teaspoon baking powder
1 teaspoon baking soda
2 teaspoons cinnamon
½ teaspoon allspice
¼ teaspoon nutmeg
*1½ cups grated zucchini
    (either fresh or frozen)*
*½ cup water, as needed if
    using fresh zucchini*

4. Spoon batter into greased muffin tins, about ¾ full. Bake for 20 to 25 minutes.

5. For bread, use two greased pans (8½ x 4½ x 2¾ inches) and bake the bread at 325°F for 1 hour.

Makes 24 muffins or 2 loaves of bread

Banana Muffins

6 ripe bananas
1 cup cooking oil
4 eggs
2 cups sugar
1½ cups tapioca flour
½ cup brown rice flour
¾ cup potato starch
¾ cup sorghum flour
¼ cup corn flour
1 tablespoon xanthan gum
*1 tablespoon plus 1 teaspoon
    baking powder*
½ teaspoon salt

These muffins freeze well.

1. Preheat oven to 400°F.

2. Use a blender to mix the bananas, oil, and eggs at high speed until smooth.

3. Combine the dry ingredients in a mixing bowl.

4. Add mixture in blender to dry ingredients and combine. (Over beating the batter will cause the texture of the muffins to be tough.)

5. Spoon batter into greased muffin tins, about ¾ full. Bake for 20 to 25 minutes.

6. For bread, use two greased pans (8½ x 4½ x 2 ⅝-inch) and bake the bread at 325°F for 45 to 55 minutes.

Makes 26 to 28 muffins or 2 loaves of bread

Buttermilk Baking-Powder Biscuits

1 cup mashed potatoes,
*   prepared from dehydrated*
*   potatoes*
2 tablespoons butter
1 cup tapioca flour
¾ cup brown rice flour
¼ cup potato starch
2 teaspoons baking powder
½ teaspoon baking soda
½ teaspoon salt
½ teaspoon xanthan gum
¾ cup buttermilk
1 egg

1. Prepare mashed potatoes according to the directions on the package. Add extra butter. The potatoes should be moist, creamy, and easily stirred, but not runny. Set aside.

2. Combine tapioca flour, brown rice flour, potato starch, baking powder, baking soda, salt, and xanthan gum in a large mixing bowl.

3. Beat milk and egg in a small mixing bowl.

4. Add the egg–buttermilk mixture to the potato mixture and beat until smooth.

5. Add this mixture to the dry ingredients and mix lightly but well.

6. Preheat oven to 400°F.

7. Lay out a large piece of plastic wrap on the kitchen counter. Place half of the dough on it and then cover with another large piece of plastic wrap. Roll out the dough that is placed between the plastic wrap until it is smooth and almost 1 inch thick.

8. Remove the top sheet of plastic wrap and cut biscuits with a biscuit cutter or a drinking glass. Place on a lightly greased cookie sheet. Repeat with the remaining dough.

9. Bake biscuits for 13 to 15 minutes. These biscuits will not brown a lot on the top, so lift one up to see if they are browned on the bottom.

Makes 8 to 9 biscuits

Our Favorite Rolls

½ cup lukewarm water

2 teaspoons yeast

2 teaspoons sugar

¾ cup milk

½ cup buttermilk (or 1¼ cups soy or almond milk)

2 cups brown rice flour

1½ cups tapioca flour

⅛ cup sugar

2½ teaspoons xanthan gum

½ cup dried potato flakes

1 teaspoon salt

½ cup cooking oil or shortening

2 tablespoons butter

2 eggs

1. Preheat oven to 170°F or warm setting.

2. To make yeast mixture, pour lukewarm water into a small bowl, then sprinkle yeast and sugar across the top of the water. Set aside. (To be sure the water is not too hot, put a couple of drops on the inside of your wrist.)

3. Microwave milk and buttermilk for about 1 minute, or until hot.

4. Combine flours, sugar, xanthan gum, potato flakes, and salt in a large bowl.

5. Fold yeast mixture, hot milk, oil, butter, and eggs into dry ingredients. Beat at high speed for 3 minutes. A heavy-duty kitchen mixer is recommended.

6. Spray muffin tins with cooking spray. Spoon dough into muffin tins, around ¾ full.

7. Set muffin tray on open oven door to rise, with oven preheated to 170°F. Let rise for approximately 20 minutes for rapid-rise yeast, and 30 minutes for regular yeast.

8. Place rolls in oven and turn heat up to 375°F. Bake for 20 to 24 minutes.

Makes 16 to 18 rolls

Tip: Rolls can be frozen if wrapped in plastic wrap and placed in a sealed freezer bag.

Cream Cheese Rolls

8 ounces cream cheese
¾ cup brown sugar
1½ teaspoons cinnamon
1½ teaspoons nutmeg

Glaze

1 tablespoon butter
1 cup powdered sugar
2 tablespoons water
½ teaspoon almond extract
½ teaspoon butter extract

1. Using recipe on page 37, make dough for Our Favorite Rolls.

2. Fill greased muffin tins about half full with dough.

3. Mix cream cheese with brown sugar, cinnamon, and nutmeg. Scoop mixture into a small plastic freezer bag.

4. Cut a ½-inch diagonal opening in one corner of the bag. Holding the bag upright, squeeze cream cheese mixture onto roll dough.

5. Add roll dough to cover the cream cheese mixture and fill the muffin tins to around ¾ full.

6. Set muffin tray on open oven door to rise, with oven preheated to 170°F. Let rise for approximately 20 minutes for rapid-rise yeast, and 30 minutes for regular yeast.

7. Place rolls in oven and turn heat up to 375°F. Bake for 20 to 24 minutes.

8. Mix glaze ingredients together and pour over hot rolls.

Makes 16 to 18 rolls

Cinnamon Rolls

¾ cup brown sugar
¼ cup sugar
1½ teaspoons cinnamon

1. Using recipe on page 37, make dough for Our Favorite Rolls.

2. Fill greased muffin tins about ½ full with roll dough.

3. Sprinkle one tablespoon of cinnamon sugar on each roll.

4. Add dough to fill the muffin tins about ¾ full. Sprinkle with additional cinnamon sugar.

5. Set muffin tray on open oven door to rise, with oven preheated to 170°F. Let rise for approximately 20 minutes for rapid-rise yeast, and 30 minutes for regular yeast.

6. Place rolls in oven and turn heat up to 375°F. Bake for 20 to 24 minutes.

7. Cover the rolls with caramel syrup (see page 21) before serving.

Makes 16 to 18 rolls

Breadsticks

*2 teaspoons Italian
    seasoning*
garlic salt
Parmesan cheese

1. Using recipe on page 37, make dough for Our Favorite Rolls. Add Italian seasoning to the dough.

1. Scoop dough into a large plastic freezer bag.

2. Cut a ½-inch diagonal opening in one corner. Holding the bag upright, squeeze a line of dough onto a greased cookie sheet.

3. Sprinkle breadsticks lightly with garlic salt and Parmesan cheese.

4. Bake for 14 to 18 minutes.

Serves 6 to 8

Butter-Topped Bread

Mashed Potatoes

1⅓ cups water
½ teaspoon salt
⅔ cup butter
½ cup milk
*1⅓–1½ cups dried potato
    flakes*

This bread is especially good when it is hot. It can be frozen in individual slices to use for French toast, or sandwiches, or to toast and serve with a creamed cheese sauce or chicken sauce. Place each slice in an individual sandwich bag and the bagged slices together in a heavy-duty ziptop plastic bag. Place them in the freezer in a bread pan to prevent the slices from breaking.

1. Put 1⅓ cups water, ½ teaspoon salt, ⅔ cup butter and ½ milk into a saucepan and bring to a boil.

Bread

2 cups lukewarm water
3 tablespoons plus 2
*   teaspoons sugar*
2 teaspoons dry yeast
*   granules*
4 eggs, well beaten
2 cups mashed potatoes
*   (see above)*
4 cups brown or white
*   rice flour*
1⅓ cups potato starch
⅔ cup tapioca flour
½ cup dry milk powder
2 teaspoons salt
1 tablespoon plus 2
*   teaspoons xanthan gum*
3 tablespoons butter

2. Remove from heat and add 1⅓ to 1½ cups dried potato flakes. The potatoes should be moist and creamy and easily stirred.

3. Measure out 2 cups of the prepared potatoes for bread. (Mashed potatoes help lessen crumbling and increase the moisture of the bread.)

4. Pour 2 cups lukewarm water into a small bowl. Sprinkle yeast and sugar over the top of the water. Set aside. Preheat oven to 350°F.

5. In a large mixing bowl, combine eggs and mashed potatoes.

6. Add dry ingredients and yeast mixture and mix well.

7. Divide dough into three greased 8½ x 4½ x 2¾-inch bread pans (larger pans will not work as well). Cover hand with a clean plastic bag and shape the dough into a loaf shape.

8. Score the center of the top of the loaf from one end to the other about ½ inch deep. Spread 1 tablespoon butter in the slit before baking.

9. Let the bread rise for 30 minutes. Bake for approximately 40 to 45 minutes. The bread should be browned on the outside and firm to touch. Overbaking will decrease the moistness of the bread.

10. Melt remaining 2 tablespoons butter. Brush the top of each hot loaf of bread with butter to soften the crust and make it easier to cut.

Makes 3 small loaves

Whole-Grain Bread

1 cup brown rice flour
½ cup brown rice flour
½ cup sorghum flour
¼ cup tapioca flour
¼ cup potato starch
⅛ cup amaranth flour
⅛ cup teff flour
¼ cup ground flax seeds
1 teaspoon salt
2 teaspoons xanthan gum
2 teaspoons instant yeast
1 cup warm water
2 tablespoons cooking oil
*2 teaspoons apple cider
    vinegar*
2 eggs, beaten
2 additional egg whites
2 tablespoons honey

1. Preheat oven to 200°F.
2. Sift dry ingredients. Combine brown rice flour, sorghum flour, tapioca flour, potato starch, amaranth flour, teff flour, flax seeds, salt, xanthan gum, and yeast.
3. Add water, cooking oil, vinegar, eggs, and honey, and mix well until lumps disappear.
4. Spoon dough into one greased 8½ x 4½ x 2¾-inch loaf pan.
5. Turn oven off and place pan in oven for 60 minutes to allow bread dough to rise.
6. Without removing bread pan, set oven temperature to 350°F. Bake 30 to 38 minutes.

Makes 1 loaf

Quick Rice Bread

3 cups brown rice flour
1½ cups potato starch
2 cups tapioca flour
¾ cup sugar
2 tablespoons xanthan gum
*1½ tablespoons baking
    powder*
1½ teaspoons salt

This bread is great for French toast, cinnamon toast, or served with butter and honey.

Rice bread is best on the day it is made because it goes stale quickly. Once bread has cooled it can be frozen.

1. Preheat oven to 375°F.

3 cups milk or soy milk

6 eggs

¾ cup cooking oil

1 teaspoon vanilla

2. In kitchen mixer, combine dry ingredients.

3. Add wet ingredients, beginning with milk, and mix for 45 seconds on medium speed.

4. Spray or grease bread pans.

5. Spoon soft dough into three small (8½ x 4½ x 2¾-inch) loaf pans. Do not press dough down.

6. Bake at 375°F for 38 to 43 minutes. Bread will be puffed up and not completely smooth on the top. It should be well browned on the sides and top, or it will be condensed and sticky in the middle.

7. Remove bread from bread pans and place on wire rack. Allow to cool for 5 to 10 minutes before covering with clean dish towels or paper towels.

8. When bread has completely cooled, wrap slices in plastic wrap and place in a sealed freezer bag to preserve moistness.

Makes 3 loaves

Cinnamon Sugar Bread

3 eggs

1 tablespoon apple cider vinegar

⅓ cup cooking oil

1 cup brown sugar

½ cup sugar

2 teaspoons cinnamon

1½ cups buttermilk, warmed

1 teaspoon salt

1 tablespoon xanthan gum

⅓ cup cornstarch

½ cup potato starch

½ cup soy flour

2 cups brown rice flour

1 tablespoon active dry yeast

1 cup raisins (optional)

1. Preheat oven to 350°F.

2. Combine eggs, vinegar, oil, sugars, cinnamon, and buttermilk in a large mixing bowl.

3. Add remaining ingredients and mix for 3 minutes.

4. Scoop dough into a greased 8½ x 4 ½ x 2¾-inch loaf pan. Bake for 38 to 42 minutes.

Quinoa Bread

1 cup brown rice flour
1 cup teff flour
½ cup tapioca flour
½ cup quinoa flakes
¼ cup potato starch
⅓ cup sugar
1 teaspoon salt
1 tablespoon xanthan gum
1½ tablespoons yeast
1¾ cups warm water
¼ cup cooking oil
1 teaspoon apple cider
* vinegar*
½ cup reconstituted potatoes
* from dried potato flakes*
3 eggs, beaten

1. Sift potato starch, if needed.

2. Combine brown rice flour, teff flour, tapioca flour, quinoa flakes, potato starch, sugar, salt, and xanthan gum in a large mixing bowl.

3. Sprinkle yeast over the combined dry ingredients and pour warm water over the top of the yeast and let it sit for 3 to 4 minutes.

4. Add oil and vinegar and mix on low speed.

5. According to package directions, make ½ cup mashed potatoes from dried potato flakes.

6. Add beaten eggs and reconstituted potatoes to mixing bowl. Beat on high speed for 3 to 5 minutes. Batter will be stiff.

7. Spoon dough into two small (8½ x 4½ x 2¾-inch) bread pans. Pat dough with spoon until smooth.

8. Let dough sit for about 20 minutes in a warm place until it has risen 1 inch. While dough is rising preheat oven to 400°F.

9. Place pans in oven and immediately reduce temperature to 350°F. Bake for 30 to 35 minutes. Bread will be very dense.

Makes 2 loaves

Tip: Quinoa is a complete protein with significant amounts of iron, potassium, and magnesium. Teff is rich in iron, calcium, and fiber.

Moist Cornbread

1 cup butter

1 cup sugar

4 eggs

16-ounce can creamed corn

4-ounce can green chilies (optional)

½ cup shredded cheddar cheese (optional)

¾ cup rice flour

¼ cup tapioca flour

½ cup gluten-free cornmeal

½ cup gluten-free corn flour

1 tablespoon plus 1 teaspoon baking powder

½ teaspoon salt

2 teaspoons xanthan gum

1. Preheat oven to 350°F.

2. Cream butter, sugar, and eggs. Add creamed corn, green chilies, and cheese.

3. Add rice flour, tapioca flour, cornmeal, corn flour, baking powder, salt, and xanthan gum.

4. Pour into a greased 9 x 13-inch baking dish. Bake for 35 to 40 minutes.

Serves 12

Tip: Earth Balance Spread® (a dairy-free margarine) is delicious and has been used successfully as a substitute for butter in the recipes in this cookbook.

Tip: Any bread that includes baking powder should be mixed only until combined.

Soups and Salads

Minestrone Soup

3 slices bacon
½ teaspoon minced garlic
1 medium onion, diced
1 stalk celery, diced
2 carrots, diced or grated
1 potato, finely diced
8 cups chicken broth
28-ounce can diced tomatoes
15-ounce can kidney beans
1 teaspoon dried basil leaves
2 teaspoons dried parsley
½ teaspoon salt
½ cup 2-inch-long uncooked
   Tinkyada® Spaghetti
   Noodle pieces
garlic salt, to taste

1. Fry bacon in a large saucepan, then remove from pan and cut into small pieces.

2. Sauté garlic, onion, celery, carrots, and potato in bacon grease for 25 minutes in same saucepan.

3. Add chicken broth and bring to a boil. Add diced tomatoes, kidney beans, basil, parsley, and salt. Simmer for 45 minutes.

4. Add uncooked noodles. Boil for 12 to 15 minutes, or until noodles are tender.

5. Season with garlic salt, to taste.

Serves 8 to 9

Italian Sausage Soup

1 pound spicy Italian
   ground sausage
14½-ounce can diced
   or stewed tomatoes
1 cup (8-ounce can) tomato
   sauce
4 cups water
1 cup gluten-free beef broth
1 large carrot, chopped

1. Place sausage in a large pot and fry until brown. Drain off excess grease.

2. Purée the stewed or diced tomatoes in a blender until smooth. Add to sausage.

3. Add water, beef broth, carrot, onion, green beans, basil, oregano, parsley, sugar, and garlic powder and bring to a boil. Reduce heat and simmer for at least 1 hour and 15 minutes.

⅓ cup chopped onion
1 can green beans, with liquid
1½ teaspoons dried basil
½ teaspoon dried oregano
1 tablespoon parsley
2 teaspoons sugar
¼ teaspoon garlic powder
1 cup gluten-free spiral or
    elbow macaroni noodles,
    uncooked
1 cup frozen peas
salt and pepper, to taste

4. Add noodles and peas and simmer an additional 15 to 20 minutes, or until pasta is tender. Add salt and pepper to taste.

Serves 7 to 9

Potato Cheese Soup

3½ cups water
2 cups diced potatoes
½ cup diced carrots
½ cup diced celery
¼ cup finely diced onion
¾ to 1 teaspoon salt, divided
½ cup butter
¼ cup brown rice flour
2 cups milk
¼ teaspoon pepper
2 cups grated cheddar
    cheese

1. Place 3½ cups water and ½ teaspoon salt in a large saucepan. Gently boil potatoes, carrots, celery, and onions in salted water until tender.

2. Drain vegetables, reserving 1 cup of vegetable water.

3. Melt butter in large saucepan. Add rice flour and stir well.

4. Add milk, ¼ to ½ teaspoon salt, and pepper, and cook over medium-high heat until mixture thickens, stirring often.

5. Add cheese and cooked vegetables. Add ½ cup of water saved from cooking vegetables, and stir well.

6. Continue adding water, ¼ cup at a time, until desired consistency is reached.

Serves 3 to 4

Baked Potato Soup

4 large baked potatoes,
cooled
⅔ cup butter
⅔ cup rice flour
6 cups milk
¾ teaspoon salt
½ teaspoon pepper
4 green onions, chopped
12 slices bacon, cooked
and crumbled
1¼ cups shredded cheese
8 ounces gluten-free sour
cream

1. Peel and cube baked potatoes and set aside. Discard the skins.

2. Melt butter, add rice flour, and stir until smooth. Cook 1 minute, stirring constantly.

3. Gradually add milk. Cook over medium heat, stirring until mixture is thickened and bubbly.

4. Add potato cubes, salt and pepper, half the green onions, half the bacon, and 1 cup of cheese. Cook until heated through.

5. Remove from heat and stir in sour cream. Add more milk if soup is too thick.

6. Serve with remaining bacon, green onions, and cheese to sprinkle on top.

Serves 5 to 6

Creamy Butternut Squash Soup

2 leeks, white portion only,
chopped
1 cup chopped carrots
5 tablespoons butter
4 cups peeled and cubed
butternut squash
1 cup peeled and sliced
yellow summer squash
(or crookneck)

1. In a large pot, melt the butter. Sauté leeks and carrots in butter for about five minutes.

2. Add butternut squash, yellow squash, chicken broth, salt, basil, oregano, dry mustard, and pepper. Bring to a boil. Reduce heat, cover pot, and simmer soup for 30 to 35 minutes, or until vegetables are tender.

3. Allow soup to cool. Purée in small batches in

6 cups gluten-free chicken
    broth
2 teaspoons salt
½ teaspoon dried basil
½ teaspoon dried oregano
½ teaspoon dry ground mustard
¼ teaspoon pepper
½ cup heavy whipping cream
1 cup milk
3 tablespoons grated
    Parmesan cheese

blender, pouring into a large bowl.

4. Return soup to pot and add cream and milk. Heat on medium heat until desired temperature is reached. Do not boil.

5. Ladle into soup bowls and sprinkle each serving with Parmesan cheese.

Serves 6 to 8

Tip: Butternut squash has some similarities to pumpkins. It takes some effort to peel and cube this squash, but this soup is so worth it.

Curried Chicken Rice Soup

2 cups cooked, cubed chicken
    (may use canned chicken)
2 cups cooked long-grain rice
2 large carrots, grated
2 celery stalks, finely diced
1 small onion, chopped
¾ cup butter or margarine
½ cup brown rice flour
⅛ cup corn flour
⅛ cup sorghum flour
1 teaspoon gluten-free
    seasoned salt
1 teaspoon curry powder
three 12-ounce cans
    evaporated milk
4 cups gluten-free chicken broth

1. In large saucepan, sauté carrots, celery, and onions in butter until tender.

2. Add dry ingredients. Gradually add evaporated milk and chicken broth. Stir well.

3. Add cooked chicken and rice. Simmer until soup is thickened to desired consistency. Add more chicken broth if soup is too thick.

Serves 9 to 10

Egg Drop Soup

3 cups chicken broth
1 tablespoon cornstarch
2 tablespoons cold water
1 egg, lightly beaten
¼ cup chopped green onion
½ to 1 teaspoon salt,
    if needed

1. Bring chicken broth to a boil.

2. Mix cornstarch with 2 tablespoons cold water and add to boiling chicken broth, stirring until mixture thickens slightly.

3. Slowly pour in egg and stir gently until egg is cooked. Remove from heat. Add green onions. Add salt, if desired.

Serves 2 to 4

Clam Chowder

6.5-ounce can minced clams
1 cup finely chopped onion
1 cup finely chopped celery
2 cups chopped red potatoes
1 cup butter
¾ cup brown rice flour
4 cups milk or half-and-half
    (or 3 cups almond
    milk plus 1 cup soy milk)
1½ teaspoons salt
½ teaspoon sugar
¼ teaspoon pepper
1 teaspoon gluten-free
    chicken bouillon powder
½ teaspoon minced garlic

1. Drain clam juice into water that barely covers the vegetables. Reserve clams.

2. Simmer vegetables until tender. Do not drain.

3. Melt butter in a small saucepan and add rice flour. Stir until mixture begins to gently boil.

4. Add milk (or half-and-half or substitutes), salt, sugar, pepper, bouillon, and garlic. Stir over medium-high heat until thickened.

5. Add cream sauce and clams to the vegetables and mix well.

Serves 7 to 8

Tip: If you don't like clams, leave them out and serve as a potato soup.

Sausage Vegetable Soup

1 pound sausage

1 onion, chopped

1 bunch kale or spinach,
   washed and chopped

7 cups low-sodium chicken
   broth*

4 unpeeled potatoes, diced

½ teaspoon minced garlic

½ teaspoon dried oregano

salt and pepper, to taste

12-ounce can evaporated
   milk, or 1⅔ cups almond
   milk or soy milk

1. Fry sausage and chopped onion until cooked. Drain fat.

2. In a large pot, combine chicken broth, kale, potatoes, garlic, and seasonings. Bring to a boil.

3. Add cooked sausage and onion.

4. When potatoes are tender, add milk and serve.

Serves 7 to 8

*If using water and chicken bouillon to make broth, reduce the bouillon due to the salt level of the sausage.

Cream of Broccoli Soup

2 cups chopped broccoli

2 tablespoons cooking oil

½ onion, chopped, or 2
   tablespoons minced dried
   onion

2 cups chopped celery

2 garlic cloves, minced

¼ cup butter

½ cup rice flour

4 cups milk or half-and-half

¼ teaspoon marjoram

2 cups chicken broth

garlic salt, to taste

1. Steam broccoli until tender.

2. In frying pan, sauté onions, celery, and garlic in cooking oil until light brown and very tender.

3. In large saucepan, melt butter. Add rice flour and stir well.

4. Add milk and marjoram and bring to a gentle boil. Stir mixture with a whisk until it thickens.

5. Add cooked vegetables and chicken broth. Sprinkle with garlic salt, to taste.

Serves 5 to 6

Cream of Rice Soup

4 cups cooked rice
1 tablespoon butter
1 large onion, chopped
3 carrots, grated
3 stalks celery, grated
½ cup butter
¾ cup brown rice flour
¼ cup sorghum flour
8 cups chicken broth
1 cup milk, soy milk, or almond
   milk
1 cup cooked ham, chopped
pepper, to taste

1. In a frying pan, sauté the vegetables in 1 tablespoon butter until tender.

2. In a large pot, melt ½ cup butter. Stir in brown rice flour and sorghum flour.

3. While stirring, gradually add chicken broth.

4. Boil until thickened and add vegetables, milk, rice, ham, and pepper.

Serves 8 to 9

Potato Bean Soup

5 cups gluten-free chicken broth
3 medium potatoes, finely diced
1 tablespoon butter, melted
1 clove garlic, minced
½ cup diced celery
2 medium carrots, shredded
½ onion, chopped
½ cup sour cream
1 tablespoon brown rice flour
2 teaspoons dried dill
⅛ teaspoon pepper
15-ounce can great northern
   beans, undrained

1. Pour chicken broth in large pot and bring to boil. Add diced potatoes and turn heat down to medium high.

2. In a frying pan, stir-fry remaining vegetables in butter and garlic until tender.

3. Combine rice flour, dill, pepper and sour cream.

4. Remove chicken broth and potatoes from heat when potatoes are tender. Add vegetables and sour cream mixture to chicken broth.

5. Whisk soup until sour cream lumps disappear. Add beans.

Serves 4 to 5

Chicken or Turkey Noodle Soup

4 chicken thighs or 2 turkey thighs
2 stalks celery, chopped
¼ cup celery leaves
1 onion, chopped
¼ teaspoon garlic powder
¼ teaspoon minced garlic
garlic salt
2 cups gluten-free spaghetti noodles (break into small pieces and measure before cooking)

1. In a large saucepan, cover chicken or turkey with water.

2. Add celery, celery leaves, onion, garlic powder, minced garlic, and additional water, as needed. Boil gently for 3 hours, or until fully cooked.

3. Remove chicken or turkey from water, cool slightly, and de-bone. Strain broth.

4. Add noodles to pan and boil for around 15 minutes, or until tender.

5. Add meat to soup and bring to boil for one minute.

Serves 5 to 7

Enchilada Soup

1 medium chicken breast or ½ pound ground beef
14-ounce can chicken broth
15-ounce can corn, undrained
10-ounce can gluten-free green enchilada sauce
15-ounce can black beans, drained
tortilla chips
shredded cheese
sour cream

1. Cook and shred chicken, or fry ground beef. (Raw chicken can be added to the chicken broth and cooked before adding other ingredients).

2. Combine chicken broth, corn, green enchilada sauce, and black beans.

3. Add meat and simmer for 10 minutes. Serve with tortilla chips, shredded cheese, and sour cream.

Serves 4 to 5

Chicken Taco Soup

1 to 1½ cups diced potatoes
2 cups raw cubed chicken
4 cups water
2 teaspoons gluten-free
   chicken bouillon
½ teaspoon crushed garlic
15-ounce can black beans
14.5-ounce can stewed
   or diced tomatoes
1 cup salsa
1 teaspoon lemon juice
15-ounce can corn (optional)
shredded cheese
sour cream
tortilla chips
salsa

1. In a large saucepan, combine potatoes, chicken, water, chicken bouillon, and garlic.

2. Boil gently until potatoes are tender and chicken is fully cooked.

3. Add black beans, stewed tomatoes, salsa, lemon juice, and corn. Simmer for 10 to 20 minutes.

4. Serve with shredded cheese, sour cream, tortilla chips, and salsa.

Serves 5 to 6

Turkey Burger Soup

1 pound turkey burger or
   ground beef
4 large potatoes, diced
1 carrot, grated
15-ounce can green beans,
   drained
two 5.5-ounce cans tomato juice
1 teaspoon gluten-free beef
   bouillon
garlic salt

1. Brown turkey burger in a frying pan until completely cooked.

2. Peel and dice potatoes and place them in a large saucepan. Cover with water.

3. Grate carrots into pan and boil until potatoes and carrots are tender.

4. Add browned turkey burger, green beans, tomato juice, and bouillon. Add more beef bouillon for flavor, if needed.

5. Sprinkle with garlic salt, to taste. Simmer until heated through.

Serves 6 to 7

Corn Chowder with Sweet Potatoes

1½ cups milk
¼ cup masa or cornmeal
3 tablespoons brown rice flour
2 tablespoons tapioca flour
1 teaspoon sugar
1 tablespoon butter
½ cup finely chopped onion
2 garlic cloves, minced
¼ teaspoon ground cumin
*½ teaspoon dried oregano
    leaves*
*4 cups gluten-free chicken
    broth*
2 cups cooked, diced chicken
*1 sweet potato, peeled and
    cut into cubes*
*⅔ cup shredded Monterey
    Jack cheese*
*1½ cups frozen corn,
    unthawed*
parsley
salt and pepper, to taste

1. Mix milk, masa, brown rice flour, tapioca flour, and sugar in bowl until well combined.

2. Heat butter in a large pot over medium heat and add onion. Cook until softened, about 6 to 8 minutes. Stir in garlic, cumin, and oregano.

3. Add broth, chicken and sweet potatoes. Bring to boil, reduce heat, and simmer until the sweet potatoes are just tender, about 8 to 10 minutes.

4. Stir in milk mixture and simmer until soup thickens, about 10 minutes.

5. Add cheese and corn and cook until cheese melts. Sprinkle with parsley and season with salt and pepper.

Serves 7 to 9

Beef Taco Soup

1 pound ground beef
1 onion, chopped
15-ounce can corn, undrained
15-ounce can kidney beans,
    drained and rinsed
two 14.5-ounce cans diced
    tomatoes
1 cup water
1 package gluten-free taco
    seasoning mix (or use
    the following:
    1 tablespoon chili
    powder, ½ teaspoon
    garlic powder, 1
    teaspoon onion powder,
    ½ teaspoon cumin, and
    salt and pepper to taste)
tortilla chips
shredded cheese

1. In a large saucepan, cook ground beef with onion until meat is browned and cooked through.

2. Add corn, beans, tomatoes, water, and seasoning mix. Simmer for 10 to 20 minutes.

3. Serve with tortilla chips and shredded cheese.

Serves 6 to 7

Savory Leek Soup

3 leeks (white portion only),
    chopped
1 onion, chopped
4 tablespoons butter

1. In a medium saucepan, sauté leeks and onion in butter until soft.

2. Add chicken broth, carrots, potatoes, and sugar. Simmer until vegetables are tender.

3. Remove from heat and allow soup to cool slightly. Purée soup in small batches in a blender,

6 cups gluten-free chicken
    broth
3 carrots, sliced
3 potatoes, diced
½ teaspoon sugar
⅓ cup cooked, crumbled
    bacon
1 cup cream
salt and pepper, to taste

pouring into a large bowl.

4.   Return puréed soup to saucepan and place on the stove. Add bacon and cream. Reheat soup over medium heat. Add salt and pepper, to taste.

Serves 5 to 7

Fact: Leeks are from the onion family and look like large green onions.

Thai Noodle Soup

2 boneless, skinless chicken
    breasts
4 packages Thai Kitchen®
    Instant Noodle Soup,
    Spring Onion flavor
6 cups water
5 teaspoons gluten-free
    chicken bouillon powder
¼ teaspoon ground ginger
¼ teaspoon minced fresh
    garlic
chopped cilantro
sliced green onions

1.   Bake chicken breasts for 45 minutes at 350°F, or boil in water for 50 to 60 minutes. Cool chicken slightly, then dice.

2.   Prepare Thai noodles according to package directions. Add 2 cups of extra water to equal 6 cups.

3.   Add cooked chicken, ginger, and garlic.

4.   Top soup with chopped cilantro and sliced green onions, if desired.

Serves 4 to 5

White Bean and Chicken Soup

two 15-ounces cans great
  northern beans
6 cups gluten-free chicken
  broth
15-ounce can hominy
½ cup chopped onions
½ teaspoon minced garlic
4-ounce can diced green
  chilies
½ teaspoon salt
½ teaspoon cumin
½ teaspoon dried oregano
⅛ teaspoon ground cayenne
  pepper
2 cups cooked, diced
  chicken, or 1 can of
  chicken
sour cream
Monterey Jack cheese

1. In a large pot, combine beans, chicken broth, hominy, onions, garlic, and green chilies. Simmer for one hour.

2. Add salt, cumin, oregano, and cayenne. Simmer soup for 30 minutes.

3. Add chicken to soup and heat through.

4. Serve soup with sour cream and shredded cheese.

Serves 5 to 7

Broccoli Cheese Soup

2 cups fresh or frozen
  broccoli (or Normandy
  mix—broccoli, cauliflower,
  and carrots)
½ cup butter, melted
½ cup brown rice flour

1. In a large pot, boil vegetables gently in water until tender. Save the vegetable water to thin the soup as needed.

2. In a saucepan over low heat, stir brown rice flour into melted butter to make a thick paste.

2 cups whole milk

1 tablespoon gluten-free
   chicken bouillon powder

¼ teaspoon pepper

1½ cups shredded cheddar
   or Colby Jack cheese

2 cups chicken broth, as
   needed

Add milk, bouillon, and pepper, stirring constantly. After the sauce thickens, sprinkle in grated cheese.

3. Add sauce to cooked vegetables in soup pot. Add chicken broth and reserved vegetable water until soup reaches desired thickness. Warm soup slowly. Do not boil.

Serves 5 to 7

Best Cream of Tomato Soup

4 cups diced canned tomatoes

1⅓ cups gluten-free chicken
   broth

2 tablespoons butter

3 tablespoons sugar

2 tablespoons chopped
   onion, green onions, or
   minced dried onion

¼ teaspoon baking soda

2 cups heavy whipping
   cream or half-and-half

2 fresh tomatoes, peeled and
   diced

1. In a medium saucepan, combine canned tomatoes, chicken broth, butter, sugar, onion, and baking soda. Simmer for 30 minutes.

2. Heat cream or half-and-half in a double boiler or microwave and add slowly to the tomato mixture. Add fresh tomatoes and serve.

Serves 5 to 7

Sensational Tomato Basil Soup

*14½-ounce can stewed
    tomatoes (not Italian)*
3½ cups milk
pinch of baking soda
3 tablespoons butter
¼ teaspoon garlic powder
½ teaspoon garlic salt
¼ teaspoon onion salt
*½ teaspoon Italian
    seasoning*
1 teaspoon dried basil
*¼ teaspoon dry ground
    mustard*
1 tablespoon sour cream
1 tablespoon cream cheese
salt and pepper, to taste

1. Purée stewed tomatoes in blender and pour into medium saucepan over medium heat.

2. Microwave milk until it comes to a boil. Remove carefully from microwave (use hot pads).

3. Bring stewed tomatoes to a boil, then add a pinch of baking soda (this keeps the milk from curdling).

4. Add milk, butter, garlic powder, garlic salt, onion salt, Italian seasoning, basil, mustard powder, sour cream, and cream cheese. Stir well. Season with salt and pepper.

Serves 4 to 5

Russian Borscht

2 cups gluten-free beef broth
4 cups water
2 potatoes, peeled and diced
¾ cup diced carrots
2 bay leaves
3 beets
cooking oil
garlic salt
½ pound ground beef

1. Pour beef broth and water into a saucepan. Add potatoes, carrots, and bay leaves and bring to a boil.

2. Peel beets and slice them into long, thin pieces. Sauté beets in cooking oil and sprinkle them with garlic salt.

3. Combine ground beef with egg and onion. Sprinkle lightly with salt and pepper and mix well. Make small meatballs and add to

1 egg
½ cup finely chopped onion
salt and pepper
2 cups shredded cabbage
1 teaspoon fresh or dried
*   dill*
sour cream

vegetables in saucepan.

4. Add cabbage and dill. Boil until meat is completely cooked (about 10 to 15 minutes) and all vegetables are tender.

5. Add beets, then boil soup for an additional minute. Remove bay leaves. Serve soup with sour cream.

Serves 6 to 8

Fiesta Soup

2 turkey drumsticks
½ cup grated carrots
1 cup grated zucchini
15-ounce can green
*   beans, drained*
¼ teaspoon dried basil
1 teaspoon garlic salt
½ teaspoon salt
1 teaspoon pepper
1½ cups gluten-free
*   spaghetti noodles (break*
*   into small pieces and*
*   measure before cooking)*

1. Place drumsticks in a large saucepan and cover with water. Boil gently until cooked, about 2½ hours.

2. Remove meat from bones and cut into small pieces. Set aside.

3. Strain broth and return to pot. Add water and chicken bouillon, if needed, to equal 2 quarts of broth.

4. Add carrots, zucchini, green beans, basil, garlic salt, salt, and pepper. Bring to a boil. Cover and reduce heat to medium. Cook 15 minutes.

5. Add gluten-free noodles and cook until tender.

6. Stir in cooked turkey.

Serves 5 to 7

Mix for Easy Cream Soup

2 cup nonfat dry milk
¾ cup cornstarch
¼ cup gluten-free chicken
*   bouillon*
2 tablespoons minced dried
*   onion*
½ garlic powder

1. Combine ingredients in a ziptop plastic bag and mix well.

2. Store the soup mix in an airtight container until ready to use.

Substituting mix for 1 can of cream soup:

1. Combine ⅓ cup mix with 1¼ cup cold water in small saucepan.

2. Cook and stir on stovetop (or use glass bowl and cook in microwave) until thickened. Allow mixture to cool before adding to recipe.

3. Add thickened mixture to casseroles as you would a can of soup. Add mushrooms and chicken, if desired.

Tip: Make ahead to allow time to thicken before using in a recipe.

Ranch Dressing

4 cups gluten-free mayonnaise
1 cup buttermilk
1 cup milk
1 tablespoon plus 1
*   teaspoon parsley*
1 tablespoon plus 1 teaspoon
*   onion powder*
½ teaspoon garlic powder
1½ teaspoons salt
1 teaspoon pepper

1. Combine ingredients and stir with wire whisk until smooth.
2. This dressing will stay fresh for several weeks. Stir well before serving.

Macaroni Shrimp Salad

4 to 5 cups gluten-free spiral
*   noodles, cooked*
2 tablespoons butter
1 teaspoon minced garlic
10 medium or large
*   uncooked shrimp,*
*   washed, peeled, and*
*   deveined*
¼ cup sliced green onions
⅓ cup sliced black olives
1 stalk celery, cut down
*   center and sliced*
½ cup mayonnaise
½ teaspoon mustard

1. Boil pasta. Allow to cool.
2. Melt butter in frying pan and add garlic. Add shrimp and cook until they turn from blue to pink. Slice shrimp into small pieces.
3. Add shrimp, green onion, olives, and celery to pasta.
4. Combine mayonnaise and mustard and add to pasta mixture and stir until well mixed. Chill before serving.

Serves 4 to 6

Artichoke Salad

2 small yellow summer
　　squash, peeled and sliced
6.5-ounce jar marinated
　　artichoke hearts, drained
　　and cut into small chunks
¼ cup cooked, crumbled bacon
1 cup sliced fresh mushrooms
3 tablespoons grated
　　Parmesan cheese
⅓ cup olive oil
1 tablespoon apple cider
　　vinegar
2 tablespoons fresh lemon
　　juice
1 teaspoon onion powder
1 teaspoon salt
½ teaspoon gluten-free
　　Worcestershire sauce
¼ teaspoon pepper
½ teaspoon sugar
½ teaspoon dried basil
½ teaspoon dried oregano
　　leaves
½ teaspoon dry ground
　　mustard
3 to 4 cups torn romaine
　　lettuce
2 tablespoons parsley
garlic salt, to taste

1. In a medium bowl, place squash, artichoke hearts, bacon, mushrooms, and Parmesan cheese.

2. To make the dressing, mix oil, vinegar, lemon juice, onion powder, salt, Worcestershire sauce, pepper, sugar, basil, oregano and dry mustard in a blender.

3. Add dressing to artichoke mixture. Chill.

4. Before serving, add romaine lettuce, parsley, and garlic salt.

Serves 4 to 6

Banana Pepper and Olive Salad

1 bag mixed salad greens
½ cup grilled, sliced chicken breast
½ cup chopped olives
½ cup grape tomatoes
¼ cup chopped green onions
4 chopped sweet banana wax peppers
¼ cup chopped artichoke hearts
freshly grated Parmesan or Romano cheese

Italian Dressing

½ cup mayonnaise
⅓ cup apple cider vinegar
1 teaspoon vegetable or olive oil
2 tablespoons corn syrup
2 tablespoons Parmesan cheese
3 tablespoons Romano cheese
¼ teaspoon garlic salt
½ teaspoon Italian seasoning
½ teaspoon parsley flakes
1 tablespoon lemon juice

1. To prepare salad, place salad greens, chicken, olives, tomatoes, green onions, peppers, and artichokes in a large bowl and toss.

2. Combine dressing ingredients in blender.

3. Add a portion of the dressing to the salad, just until coated. Save remaining dressing for future use.

4. Before serving salad, add freshly grated cheese.

Serves 6 to 8

Elegant Rice Salad

3 cups cooked rice

½ cup marinated chopped
   artichoke hearts

⅓ cup green onions, sliced

¼ cup grape tomatoes

1 cup frozen peas

½ cup diced red pepper

½ cup diced green pepper

½ cup diced yellow pepper

¼ cup slivered almonds

½ cup canola oil

½ cup Parmesan cheese

1 teaspoon salt

¼ teaspoon black pepper

¼ teaspoon paprika

3 tablespoons apple cider
   vinegar

1 tablespoon sugar

½ teaspoon garlic salt

½ teaspoon dry ground
   mustard

½ teaspoon garlic powder

1. Combine rice with artichokes, green onions, tomatoes, peas, peppers, and almonds.

2. To make the dressing, purée oil, cheese, salt, pepper, paprika, vinegar, sugar, garlic salt, dry ground mustard, and garlic powder in a blender.

3. Add dressing to salad and mix well.

Serves 5 to 7

Exceptional Strawberry Salad

*6-ounce bag pre-washed
    spinach*
1 cup cooked, diced chicken
⅓ cup cooked, crumbled bacon
¼ cup cashew pieces
¼ cup sliced green onions
1 cup sliced strawberries
*½ cup sweetened dried
    cranberries*
*½ cup grated Parmesan or
    Romano cheese*
*2 tablespoons apple cider
    vinegar*
3 tablespoons sugar
½ cup olive oil
*½ teaspoon dry ground
    mustard*
½ teaspoon salt
½ cup strawberry jam

1. In a large bowl, combine spinach, chicken, bacon, cashew pieces, green onions, strawberries, and cranberries.

2. To make the dressing, purée vinegar, sugar, oil, dry ground mustard, salt, and strawberry jam in a blender.

3. Add dressing to salad just before serving and top with grated cheese.

Serves 6 to 8

Pear Romaine Salad

1½ teaspoon apple cider vinegar
1 tablespoon olive oil
½ teaspoon sugar
1½ cups romaine salad mix
1 pear, sliced
¼ cup cashews
⅛ cup cooked, crumbled bacon

1. Combine vinegar, oil, and sugar.

2. Toss dressing with salad mix, pear, cashews, and bacon.

Serves 1

Grilled Chicken and Vegetable Salad

1 pound chicken
1 pound shrimp
2 green bell peppers, diced
6 stalks of asparagus, cut
  into small pieces
4 cups Romaine and iceberg
  lettuce
1 medium tomato, diced
1 avocado, diced
½ cup olive oil
¼ cup fresh lemon juice
½ teaspoon sugar
1 ½ teaspoons dried basil
¼ teaspoon salt
⅛ teaspoon pepper

1. Prepare dressing before starting salad. Combine olive oil, lemon juice, sugar, basil, salt, and pepper. Refrigerate dressing for at least ½ hour before serving salad.

2. Fry or grill chicken and shrimp and dice into small pieces.

3. Sauté bell peppers and asparagus in cooking oil until tender. Toss with lettuce leaves, tomato, and avocado.

4. Add chicken and shrimp.

5. Pour dressing over salad just before serving.

Serves 5 to 6

Corn Chip Salad

15-ounce can kidney beans,
  drained
1 green pepper, diced
3 green onions, with tops,
  finely chopped
2 tomatoes, diced
1 small bag of Fritos R *or*
  other gluten-free corn chips
Kraft R *Catalina salad*
  dressing

1. Combine kidney beans, green pepper, green onions, and tomatoes.

2. Just before serving add dressing and toss until coated, then add corn chips and toss again.

Serves 5 to 7

Bacon Avocado Salad

5 cups romaine lettuce
½ cup marinated, chopped
  artichoke hearts
1 avocado, chopped
⅛ cup cooked, crumbled bacon
½ cup grape tomatoes
⅛ cup grated Parmesan cheese
ranch dressing

1. Place lettuce, artichoke hearts, avocado, bacon, tomatoes, and Parmesan cheese in a large serving bowl.
2. Serve with ranch dressing.

Serves 4 to 6

Broccoli Salad

1 bunch broccoli, diced
½ cup raisins
⅛ cup bacon pieces
½ cup sunflower seeds
⅛ cup diced red onions
½ cup sliced fresh mushrooms
1 cup mayonnaise
½ cup sugar
3 tablespoons milk or soy milk
½ tablespoon apple cider vinegar

1. Chop broccoli into small pieces.
2. Add raisins, bacon pieces, sunflower seeds, red onions, and mushrooms.
3. Make dressing by mixing mayonnaise, sugar, milk, and vinegar. Add to broccoli mixture and toss.

Serves 6 to 8

Southwestern Salad

1 bag mixed salad greens
½ cup black beans
½ cup chopped tomatoes
¼ cup chopped green onions
½ cup shredded cheddar cheese
½ cup cooked corn, drained
mango salsa or chopped mango
1 cup diced, cooked chicken
cumin, to taste
salt, to taste
tortilla chips
1 cup ranch dressing
2 tablespoons gluten-free
  barbeque sauce

1. In a large bowl, combine salad greens, beans, tomatoes, green onions, cheese, corn, mango salsa, chicken, cumin, and salt.

2. To make the dressing, combine ranch dressing and barbecue sauce in a small bowl.

3. Add dressing to salad and toss until coated, then add tortilla chips and toss again. Serve immediately.

Serves 6 to 8

Greek Salad

3 cups romaine lettuce, torn
1 cucumber, diced
1 tomato, chopped
½ cup sliced red onion
¼ cup feta cheese
2 tablespoons olive oil
2 tablespoons fresh lemon juice
1 teaspoon dried oregano
½ teaspoon salt

1. Combine lettuce and vegetables. Top salad with feta cheese.

2. To make the dressing, mix olive oil, lemon juice, oregano, and salt in a blender. Pour dressing over salad and toss.

Serves 3 to 4

Spinach Salad

4 cups iceberg lettuce
4 cups fresh spinach
½ cup sliced almonds
3 tablespoons sugar
½ tablespoon butter
¼ cup green onions,
    chopped, or thinly sliced
    red onion
½ cup mushrooms, sliced
2 tablespoons grated
    Parmesan or Swiss
    cheese
2 tablespoons bacon pieces
1 can mandarin oranges,
    drained

1. Tear lettuce and spinach into small pieces.
2. Sauté sliced almonds in sugar and butter until sugar dissolves and almonds turn light brown.
3. Combine lettuce and spinach with almonds and remaining salad ingredients.
4. Serve with poppyseed dressing. Recipe below.

Serves 7 to 8

Poppyseed Dressing

⅓ cup apple cider vinegar
2 teaspoons poppyseeds
½ teaspoon salt
½ cup sugar
½ teaspoon onion powder
½ tablespoon mustard
1 cup olive oil

This dressing is also excellent with steamed vegetables such as broccoli, cauliflower, carrots, and spinach.

1. Blend apple cider vinegar, poppyseeds, salt, sugar, and onion powder until sugar is dissolved.
2. Add oil. Mix well.

Taco Salad

1 pound ground beef
1 tablespoon gluten-free taco seasoning mix
2 cups gluten-free corn chips
4 cups chopped lettuce or salad mix
1 large tomato, chopped
1 cup grated cheese
½ cup black beans or gluten-free chili (optional)

1. Cook the ground beef and drain the fat.
2. Season the ground beef with taco mix. Cool slightly.
3. Warm the beans or chili. Combine all ingredients.
4. Serve immediately with ranch dressing and salsa.

Serves 4 to 5

Tip: Non-dairy Tofutti® American Cheese Slices, cut into strips, may be substituted for grated cheese.

Chicken Pasta Salad

3 cups uncooked gluten-free spiral noodles
2 chicken breasts, cooked and diced
¼ cup chopped green onions
¾ cup pineapple tidbits drained
½ cup chopped celery
1 cup red grapes, cut in half
1 can water chestnuts, chopped
½ cup salted cashews
¼ cup sweetened dried cranberries
1 cup mayonnaise
1 cup coleslaw dressing

1. Cook and drain pasta.
2. Add chicken, onions, pineapple, celery, grapes, chestnuts, cashews, and cranberries.
3. Blend mayonnaise and coleslaw dressing and add to salad. Mix well and chill.

Serves 7 to 9

Chicken Cabbage Salad

2 boneless, skinless chicken
   breasts
¼ cup brown sugar
½ head of cabbage, sliced
3 green onions, sliced
1 tablespoon butter
¼ cup slivered almonds
2 tablespoons sugar
cooking oil
1 tablespoon mayonnaise
1 teaspoon molasses
1 tablespoon gluten-free soy
   sauce
½ tablespoon apple cider vinegar
½ teaspoon salt

1. Fry chicken breasts in 2 teaspoons cooking oil, then dice chicken and return it to pan. Add brown sugar and soy sauce, stirring until sugar dissolves.

2. Fry almonds in butter and sugar until they turn light golden brown. Cool slightly.

3. Place cabbage in salad bowl with green onions. Add caramelized almonds and cooked chicken and mix well.

4. Mix 1½ tablespoons oil, mayonnaise, molasses, vinegar, and salt. Pour over salad, then toss.

Serves 4 to 6

Tip: One-half bag of coleslaw mix may be substituted for the cabbage.

Macaroni Salad

½ package Tinkyada® Elbow
   Noodles
¾ cup mayonnaise
½ teaspoon mustard
1 teaspoon sugar
½ teaspoon garlic salt
⅛ teaspoon pepper
½ onion or 2 green onions,
   chopped
2 hard-boiled eggs, diced
1 dill pickle, finely diced

1. Cook elbow noodles until tender.

2. Combine mayonnaise with mustard, sugar, garlic salt, and pepper in a small bowl and add to drained noodles.

3. Add onion, eggs, and pickle to sauce and noodles. Stir well. Mix well again before serving.

Serves 5 to 7

Tasty Sweet Pork Mexican Salad

Sweet Pork

2½ pounds pork (roast or
country spare ribs)
3 cups water
½ teaspoon garlic salt
½ teaspoon salt
½ teaspoon pepper
½ cup gluten-free green chili
sauce
¾ cup brown sugar

Salad

1 gluten-free corn tortilla
per serving
⅓ cup Mexican blend grated
cheese per tortilla
cooked rice
sweet pork
chopped lettuce
*Fritos*ᴿ *or other gluten-free*
corn chips
black beans, chilled and
drained
corn, chilled and drained
fresh salsa (see page 77)

1. Put pork, water, salt, garlic salt, and pepper in slow cooker. Cover and cook on high for 4 hours.

2. Remove pork from slow cooker and shred. Drain all but 1½ cups water from slow cooker. Stir green chili sauce and brown sugar into water in slow cooker, then add pork. Cook on LOW for an additional 2 to 3 hours.

3. While pork is cooking, make salad dressing. Combine ingredients in blender and mix at high speed.

4. When pork and rice are ready, sprinkle ⅓ cup cheese on each corn tortilla and place in a 300°F oven for 2 to 5 minutes or until cheese melts, or place in a frying pan until corn tortilla is crispy.

5. Top tortilla with rice, pork, lettuce, beans, corn, corn chips, and salsa. Add dressing.

Tip: Prepare ingredient quantities above according to the number of people being served. Freeze leftover pork.

Tip: Cilantro, lime juice, and remaining Anaheim pepper and jalapeno pepper (from dressing) can be added to rice.

Dressing

*½ Anaheim pepper (remove
    seeds using gloves, if desired)*
*½ jalapeno pepper (remove
    seeds using gloves, if desired)*
*1½ cloves garlic or 1½
    teaspoons minced garlic*
*2 medium tomatillos,
    roasted or sautéed*
juice of one lime
salt, to taste
*16-ounce bottle gluten-free
    peppercorn ranch dressing,
    or two cups ranch dressing*

Fresh Salsa

*28-ounce can whole
    peeled tomatoes*
*2 teaspoons to 1 tablespoon
    chopped jalapeno*
*4-ounce can diced green
    chilies*
⅓ cup chopped fresh cilantro
¼ cup chopped onion
1 tablespoon lemon or lime juice
1 teaspoon dried oregano
2 teaspoons minced garlic
1 teaspoon salt
1 teaspoon pepper

1. Drain liquid from canned tomatoes into blender. Add remaining ingredients (except tomatoes) and liquefy.
2. Add whole tomatoes and pulse to desired consistency.

Makes about 4 cups

Favorite Potato Salad

2 hard-boiled eggs, diced
5 medium red potatoes,
    cooked and diced
1 cup mayonnaise
1 teaspoon apple cider
    vinegar
½ teaspoon mustard
1 teaspoon sugar
¼ teaspoon salt
½ teaspoon garlic salt
¼ teaspoon pepper
¼ teaspoon garlic powder
¼ teaspoon onion powder
1 cup chopped celery
¼ cup chopped green
    onions, with green tops
¼ cup chopped dill pickle

1. Combine mayonnaise, vinegar, mustard, sugar, salt, garlic salt, pepper, garlic powder, and onion powder in a large bowl.
2. Add eggs, potatoes, celery, green onions, and dill pickle. Mix well.

Serves 5 to 7

Bean Salad

15-ounce can green beans,
    drained
15-ounce can yellow wax
    beans, drained
15-ounce can red kidney
    beans or garbanzo
    beans, drained
1 green pepper, diced

1. Pour drained beans into a large bowl.
2. Add diced peppers and onions and mix well.
3. Combine remaining ingredients and add to beans and vegetables. Stir well. Allow salad to marinate for 8 to 10 hours.

1 small onion, diced
¾ cup sugar
⅔ cup apple cider vinegar
⅓ cup cooking oil
2 tablespoons brown sugar
lemon pepper, to taste
garlic salt, to taste

4. Serve salad using a slotted spoon.

Serves 8 to 10

Tip: If you don't have kidney beans or garbanzos on hand, use pinto beans.

Creamy Gelatin Salad

3-ounce box raspberry gelatin
3.4-ounce box vanilla
*   pudding (not instant)*
2½ cups water
8-ounce container whipped
*   topping*
1 cup fresh strawberries

1. In a small saucepan, combine gelatin, pudding, and water. Cook over medium-high heat until mixture boils for 1 minute.

2. Transfer to a serving bowl and allow to set up in fridge for 1 to 2 hours.

3. Add whipped topping and fruit and mix well.

Serves 5 to 7

Mandarin Orange Salad

3-ounce box orange gelatin
3.4-ounce box vanilla
*   pudding (not instant)*
3.4-ounce box tapioca
*   pudding (not instant)*
3 cups water
12-ounce container
*   whipped topping*
two 11-ounce cans
*   mandarin oranges*

1. Place gelatin and pudding in a large saucepan. Add water and bring to a boil for one minute, stirring often.

2. Transfer mixture to large mixing bowl and refrigerate for 1 to 2 hours. Add whipped topping and oranges.

Serves 8 to 10

Pretzel Salad

2⅔ cups coarsely crushed
  Ener-G^ᴿ Foods Crisp
  Gluten-Free Pretzels

3 tablespoons sugar

¾ cup butter

8-ounce package cream
  cheese

1 cup sugar

4-ounce container whipped
  topping

6-ounce box raspberry or
  strawberry gelatin

2 cups boiling water

1 pint frozen raspberries or
  strawberries

1. Preheat oven to 350°F.

2. In a large bowl, cream sugar and butter together. Stir in pretzels.

3. Press mixture into a 9 x 13-inch pan and bake for 10 minutes. Allow pretzel crust to cool.

4. Combine cream cheese, sugar, and whipped topping, mixing well. Spread over crust. Refrigerate.

5. Dissolve gelatin in boiling water. Add berries. When partially set, spoon gelatin and fruit mixture over cream cheese mixture. Refrigerate salad for several hours before serving.

Serves 9 to 11

Sides

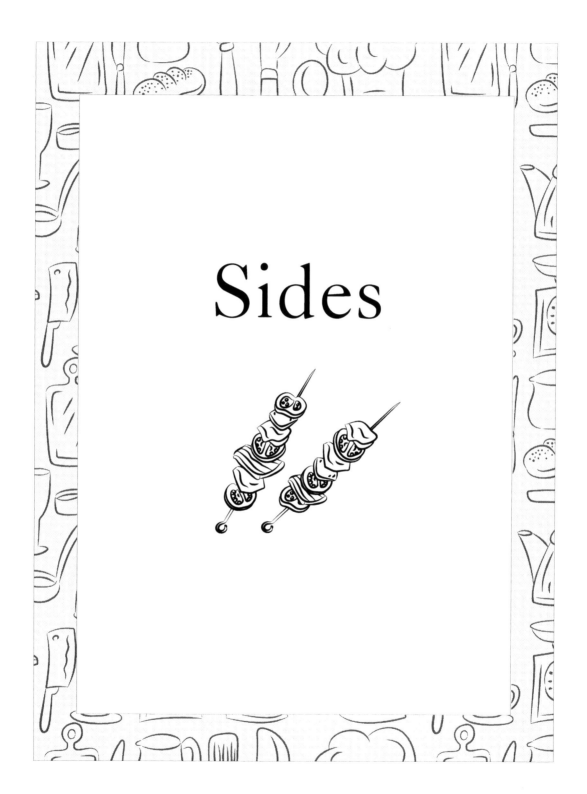

Parmesan Noodles

¼ pound bacon, cut into pieces, or 2 tablespoons precooked bacon pieces

3 tablespoons butter or margarine

2 garlic cloves, crushed, or 1 teaspoon minced garlic

1 egg

⅓ cup Parmesan cheese

½ cup chopped green onions

8 ounces gluten-free spaghetti or spiral noodles (use half of a 16-ounce package)

garlic salt, to taste

1. In a frying pan, cook bacon and pour off grease. (If using precooked bacon pieces, just place in the pan with the butter). Heat bacon with butter until butter melts. Add garlic and sauté. Remove from heat.

2. Meanwhile, in a small bowl, mix egg, Parmesan cheese, and green onions. Set aside.

3. In a large saucepan, cook the spaghetti noodles until done. Drain noodles and return them to the pan. Immediately add the Parmesan and egg mixture. Heat noodles until the egg is cooked. Add the bacon, garlic, and butter mixture to the noodles and mix well.

Serves 5 to 7

Mediterranean Pasta

2 cups cooked gluten-free pasta

¼ cup sliced green onions

3 tablespoons Italian dressing

¼ teaspoon dried basil

1½ tablespoons grated Parmesan cheese

garlic salt, to taste

Combine gluten-free pasta with remaining ingredients and serve.

Serves 2

Creamy Italian Pasta

½ cup chopped onion

2 garlic cloves, crushed, or
    1 teaspoon minced garlic

2 tablespoons olive oil

3 to 4 slices bacon, or 4
    tablespoons bacon pieces

1 large chicken breast

⅔ cup gluten-free spaghetti
    sauce

1 cup heavy whipping cream

1 teaspoon dried basil

¼ teaspoon dried parsley

¼ teaspoon dried oregano

½ teaspoon salt

¼ teaspoon pepper

16 ounces gluten-free spiral
    or fettuccini noodles

Parmesan cheese, to taste

garlic salt, to taste

1 to 2 cups fried or steamed
    garden vegetables
    (optional)

½ cup sliced, fried
    mushrooms (optional)

1. In a skillet, sauté the garlic and onion in olive oil.

2. Cut raw chicken and bacon into small pieces and add to pan. Cook over medium heat until chicken is cooked through.

3. Pour sauce and heavy whipping cream over chicken and onion. Mix well.

4. Season with basil, parsley, oregano leaves, and salt and pepper to taste.

5. Simmer the sauce over low heat for 15 minutes.

6. Cook pasta in boiling salted water while sauce simmers. Drain pasta and top with sauce and Parmesan cheese, if desired.

7. Add garlic salt, cooked garden vegetables, and mushrooms, if desired.

Serves 8 to 10

Mac and Cheese

½ package gluten-free elbow noodles
¼ cup butter
2 tablespoons milk
1½ cheese packets from Kraft Macaroni and Cheese^R (Do not eat noodles included in the box.)

1. Cook the gluten-free noodles.
2. Add butter, milk, and powdered cheese.

Serves 3 to 5

Tip: Place the Kraft noodles in a plastic bag and give them to a friend who can have food with gluten in it.

Roasted Red Potatoes

5 to 6 red potatoes
4 tablespoons olive oil
1 tablespoon dried parsley
garlic salt, to taste
onion salt, to taste
pepper, to taste

1. Preheat oven to 425°F.
2. Cut potatoes into wedges.
3. Spread 2 tablespoons oil on a shallow baking pan such as a cookie sheet or jelly-roll pan.
4. Place the potatoes in a plastic bag with 2 tablespoons oil. Squeeze and shake the bag until the oil coats the potatoes.
5. Spread the potatoes on the cookie sheet in a single layer. Sprinkle with seasonings and parsley. Bake for 30 to 40 minutes or until tender.

Serves 5 to 7

Fried Garlic Potatoes

8 small red potatoes
3 tablespoons butter
3 garlic cloves, crushed
garlic salt, to taste
onion salt, to taste

1. Steam the potatoes until tender. Allow to cool slightly.

2. Cut potatoes into large cubes, leaving skins on.

3. Melt butter in a large frying pan. Add crushed garlic.

4. Carefully add potatoes to hot butter and garlic.

5. Sprinkle with garlic salt and onion salt.

6. Cook potatoes until lightly browned.

Serves 5 to 7

Creamy Potatoes

5 potatoes
3 tablespoons butter
½ cup grated cheese
½ cup heavy whipping cream
salt and pepper
parsley

1. Peel potatoes and cut them into French fries.

2. Place potatoes in a baking dish lined with foil.

3. Season potatoes with salt and pepper. Cut butter into small pieces and drop onto potatoes.

4. Pour cream over potatoes, then sprinkle with cheese and parsley.

5. Cover with foil, sealing the edges. Bake at 425°F for 50 to 55 minutes, or until potatoes are tender.

Serves 6 to 8

Scalloped Potatoes

4 tablespoons butter

2 tablespoons brown rice flour

1 teaspoon sugar

2 to 3 teaspoons salt, to taste

½ teaspoon minced garlic

¼ teaspoon onion powder

3 cups milk

6 to 7 potatoes, thinly sliced

1 cup grated Colby Jack cheese

1. Preheat oven to 350°F.

2. Melt butter in a medium saucepan. Add brown rice flour, sugar, salt, garlic, and onion powder.

3. Gradually add milk. Whisk mixture over medium-high heat until slightly thickened.

4. Add potatoes and cook for 10 minutes, stirring constantly.

5. Pour into a greased 9 x 13-inch pan. Sprinkle with grated cheese and cover with foil.

6. Bake at 350°F for 1 hour. Remove foil and cook for 10 to 20 minutes, or until potatoes are tender.

Serves 6 to 8

Summer Squash and Bacon

1 tablespoon butter

2 cups cubed yellow summer squash

⅓ cup grated or shredded Parmesan cheese

¼ cup cooked, crumbled bacon

1 tomato, chopped

salt and pepper, to taste

1. Sauté squash in butter until tender.

2. Stir in remaining ingredients.

Serves 2 to 4

Sensational Sweet Potatoes

*3 cups cooked, mashed sweet
  potatoes*
¾ cup sugar
⅛ cup melted butter
2 eggs, well beaten
1 teaspoon vanilla
⅓ cup evaporated milk
½ cup brown sugar
¼ cup brown rice flour
½ cup pecan or almond pieces
2 tablespoons melted butter

1. Preheat oven to 350ºF. Mix cooked sweet potatoes, sugar, butter, eggs, vanilla, and evaporated milk in a medium bowl.

2. Spoon mixture into a greased 8 x 8-inch baking dish.

3. Mix remaining ingredients in a small bowl and sprinkle over sweet potato mixture. Cover and bake at 350ºF for 25 to 30 minutes.

Serves 4 to 6

Tasty Yams

*2 medium-sized yams,
  scrubbed clean*
½ cup brown sugar
⅓ cup butter
*1 cup miniature
  marshmallows (optional)*

1. Pierce yams with a fork.

2. Microwave yams for 7 to 10 minutes, or until they indent slightly when squeezed.

3. Cut yams in half and remove skins. Place in an 8 x 8-inch glass casserole dish. Mash yams with a fork to remove lumps.

4. Stir in brown sugar and butter. Microwave for 2 to 4 minutes, or until butter melts and brown sugar dissolves. Mix well.

5. If desired, cover yams with miniature marshmallows and broil in oven until they turn light brown.

Serves 4 to 6

Sesame Green Beans

2 cups cooked green beans
(can use fresh, canned,
or frozen)
½ teaspoon garlic salt
¼ teaspoon onion powder
1 to 2 tablespoons butter
1 tablespoon gluten-free soy
sauce
1 tablespoon toasted sesame
seeds

1. In a small saucepan, combine garlic salt, onion powder, butter, soy sauce, and sesame seeds. Cook, stirring frequently over medium heat, until butter is melted and sauce is hot.

2. Pour over cooked green beans.

Serves 3 to 5

Cucumbers with Vinegar

1 large cucumber, peeled
and sliced
½ cup apple cider vinegar
½ cup water
½ teaspoon garlic salt
½ teaspoon salt

This recipe is for those who love a sour and salty vinegar flavor.

1. Combine vinegar, water, garlic salt, and salt in a small serving bowl.

2. Add sliced cucumber. Marinate for several hours before serving.

Serves 2 to 3

Fried Zucchini

1 large zucchini
1 egg
1 teaspoon water
¼ cup rice flour
¼ cup corn flour or
*   cornmeal*
cooking oil
garlic salt, to taste
seasoned salt, to taste

1. Peel zucchini and cut into ⅛ to ¼-inch slices.

2. Combine egg and water in a sealable bag. Add zucchini and shake bag until egg and water coat the zucchini.

3. Mix rice flour and corn flour (or cornmeal) together in a pie plate. Dip both sides of each zucchini slice in flour mixture.

4. Coat griddle with cooking oil. Fry zucchini until golden brown on each side.

5. Season with garlic salt and seasoned salt.

Serves 6 to 8

Apple Dip

4 Fuji apples
8-ounce package cream
*   cheese*
1¼ cups brown sugar
1 teaspoon vanilla extract

1. Wash and slice apples.

2. In a serving bowl, combine cream cheese, brown sugar, and vanilla. Whip with a spoon or electric mixer until smooth and creamy.

3. Dip apples in mixture.

Serves 4 to 6

El Salvadoran Rice

1 cup white, long-grain rice (not instant rice)
¼ cup cooking oil
2 cups water
½ teaspoon gluten-free chicken bouillon
1 small onion, diced
2 carrots, grated
1 teaspoon salt
¼ teaspoon garlic salt
1 tomato, chopped
2 tablespoons chopped cilantro
onion salt, to taste

1. Place rice in frying pan with ¼ cup oil. Stir until oil is absorbed and rice is lightly browned.

2. Add water, bouillon, onion, carrots, salt, and garlic salt. Reduce heat to low, cover with lid, and simmer for 20 to 30 minutes.

3. Taste rice and if it is not soft, add more water and bouillon and simmer for several more minutes.

4. Add chopped tomatoes and cilantro before serving. Season with onion salt, to taste.

Serves 3 to 5

Zesty Italian Rice

3 cups cooked instant white rice
3 tablespoons ranch dressing
3 tablespoons Italian dressing
1 tablespoon butter
½ teaspoon lemon juice
¼ to ½ teaspoon garlic salt
¼ teaspoon dried oregano

1. Prepare instant rice according to directions. (Four servings will make about three cups of rice.) Measure cooked rice and place in medium-size serving bowl.

2. Add ranch dressing, Italian dressing, butter, lemon juice, garlic salt, and oregano. Mix well. Add additional garlic salt, if needed.

Serves 3 to 5

Italian Rice

4 cups cooked rice
½ teaspoon crushed garlic
*1 cup gluten-free spaghetti
  sauce*
½ teaspoon garlic salt
*½ cup grated mozzarella
  cheese*
*1 tablespoon Parmesan
  cheese*

Combine cooked rice, garlic, gluten-free spaghetti sauce, garlic salt, mozzarella cheese, and Parmesan cheese and heat in microwave until warm. Top with additional Parmesan cheese, if desired.

Serves 6 to 8

Spanish Rice

*1 cup white or brown rice,
  or a mixture of both*
2 cups hot water
2 tablespoons cooking oil
½ cup chopped onion
½ cup chopped green pepper
¼ cup grated carrot
1 garlic clove, minced
¼ teaspoon cumin
1 teaspoon salt
⅛ teaspoon black pepper
1 cup chopped fresh tomatoes
fresh cilantro (optional)
lime juice, to taste (optional)
garlic salt, to taste

1. Preheat oven to 350°F.
2. Place rice and water in buttered or sprayed 9 x 9-inch casserole dish. Cover with foil and bake for 50 to 60 minutes, or until water is absorbed.
3. While rice is baking, sauté the onion, carrots, and green pepper in cooking oil until tender. Add minced garlic and seasonings.
4. Place baked rice in frying pan with 2 tablespoons oil and stir well to coat with oil. Add cooked vegetables and seasonings. Heat rice mixture for several more minutes.
5. Add raw tomatoes and desired optional ingredients. Sprinkle with garlic salt.

Serves 4 to 6

Red Spanish Rice

1 medium onion, diced (or 1
   tablespoon minced dried
   onion)
1 small green pepper, diced
2 garlic cloves, crushed, or
   1 teaspoon minced garlic
2 tablespoons cooking oil
2 cups uncooked rice
4½ cups water
1 teaspoon gluten-free beef
   bouillon
14.5-ounce can diced or
   stewed tomatoes
1 tablespoon brown sugar
¼ teaspoon hot cayenne pepper
   sauce
1 teaspoon salt
¼ teaspoon pepper
1½ teaspoons chili powder
½ teaspoon cumin
1 tablespoon gluten-free
   Worcestershire sauce
½ cup cooked, crumbled
   bacon
2 to 3 tablespoons chopped
   cilantro
shredded cheese
sour cream

1. Sauté onion, green pepper, and garlic in a large frying pan in 2 tablespoons oil until tender. Add uncooked rice and mix well.

2. Add water, beef bouillon, tomatoes, brown sugar, red pepper sauce, salt, pepper, chili powder, cumin, and Worcestershire sauce. Bring to a boil and then turn heat to medium. Simmer for 30 minutes, stirring constantly. If rice is not tender, add more chicken broth or water and simmer the rice for several more minutes.

3. Before serving, stir in cilantro and bacon. Serve with grated cheese and sour cream.

Serves 5 to 7

Tip: For a delicious main dish, cook and shred a roast and add salsa, garlic, green chilies, and cooked green pepper. Place a scoop of meat on a warm corn tortilla with fresh salsa and Red Spanish Rice.

Golden Rice with Roasted Vegetables

½ cup brown rice

½ cup white rice

2 tablespoons olive oil

1 cup gluten-free chicken broth

1 cup gluten-free beef broth

1 tablespoon dried minced onion

1 tablespoon butter

garlic salt

2 cups asparagus spears, sliced into 2-inch sections (or stir-fry vegetables)

½ cup diced yellow or red peppers

½ cup chopped onion

¼ cup sliced carrots

3 tablespoons olive oil

garlic salt and pepper, to taste

sliced almonds

Parmesan cheese

crumbled feta cheese

1. In a frying pan over medium heat, toast brown and white rice with olive oil until golden brown (5 to 10 minutes).

2. Preheat oven to 350°F.

3. Spray an 8 x 8-inch baking dish with cooking spray. Add toasted rice, broth, dried minced onion, and butter. Sprinkle with garlic salt. Cover baking dish. Bake for about one hour, or until rice is no longer firm.

4. Toss asparagus, peppers, onion, and carrots in oil until coated. Add garlic salt and pepper. Bake at 400°F for 30 to 35 minutes, or until tender.

5. Combine baked rice and roasted vegetables in large serving bowl. Sprinkle with sliced almonds, Parmesan cheese, and feta cheese.

Serves 7 to 9

Fried Rice

1½ cups white rice
1½ cups brown rice
6 cups water
cooking oil
½ teaspoon minced garlic
2 eggs
3 green onions
ground ginger, to taste
garlic salt, to taste
onion salt, to taste

1. Preheat oven to 350°F.

2. Spray a 9 x 13-inch casserole dish with cooking spray.

3. Pour a thin layer of cooking oil across the bottom of the dish.

4. Pour rice and water into dish. Cover with foil. Bake for 1 hour to 1 hour and 20 minutes, or until water is absorbed.

5. When rice is cooked, pour small amount of olive oil in large, nonstick frying pan or wok until the bottom of pan is covered.

6. Add garlic, eggs, and chopped green onions and stir together.

7. When eggs are scrambled, add the cooked rice.

8. Sprinkle with small amounts of ground ginger, garlic salt, and onion salt. Mix well. Fry until rice is completely warmed.

Serves 7 to 9

Tip: The sauce for Sweet and Sour Meatballs (see page 136) is delicious with this rice.

Ham Fried Rice

½ cup white rice

½ cup brown rice

1 cup water

1 cup chicken broth

½ teaspoon salt

¼ teaspoon gluten-free
    chicken bouillon

⅛ cup butter

1 cup diced, cooked ham,
    or 3 teaspoons gluten-
    free bacon pieces

⅓ cup butter or cooking oil

½ cup chopped onion

¼ cup chopped green pepper

¼ cup diced celery

½ cup sliced fresh mushrooms
    (optional)

2 teaspoons gluten-free soy
    sauce

1 egg

1. Preheat oven to 350°F.

2. Combine rice, water, chicken broth, salt, gluten-free chicken bouillon, and butter in a 9 x 9-inch casserole dish. Cover with lid or foil and bake for 45 to 50 minutes, or until liquid is absorbed.

3. Allow rice to cool slightly while preparing ham and vegetables.

4. Heat butter or oil in a large, nonstick frying pan. Add diced ham, onion, pepper, celery, mushrooms, and soy sauce. Cook until tender, then add cooked rice and mix well.

5. Move rice and vegetable mixture to the side of the pan and place egg in the empty part of the pan. Stir egg until scrambled, then blend into rice mixture.

Serves 4 to 6

Variation: Add 1 cup finely shredded Chinese cabbage.

Savory Rice with Butter

2 cups water
2 teaspoons salt
1 cup long-grain white rice
¼ cup butter
1/8 teaspoon garlic salt
1¾ cups water
2 teaspoons gluten-free
  chicken bouillon
2 tablespoons dried parsley
½ teaspoon crushed garlic
1 tablespoon butter
¼ cup slivered almonds
¼ cup cooked, crumbled
  bacon

1. Bring water and salt to a boil in a small saucepan. Remove from heat and add rice. Let stand for 30 minutes.

2. Preheat oven to 350°F.

3. Rinse rice with cold water and drain well. Melt butter in frying pan and add rice. Cook over medium heat for 5 minutes.

4. Pour rice into greased 8 x 8-inch baking dish and sprinkle with garlic salt. Heat water and add bouillon. Stir until bouillon dissolves, then add to rice. Add parsley and crushed garlic, mixing well.

5. Cover baking dish and bake for 45 minutes. While rice is baking, melt butter in a small frying pan over medium heat. Sauté almonds in butter until they are slightly browned.

6. Add almonds to rice and bake uncovered for 10 additional minutes. Add cooked bacon and serve.

Main Dishes

Pineapple Chicken Lo Mein

1 can pineapple chunks
1 pound chicken, diced
2 cloves garlic, minced
¾ teaspoon ginger
2 tablespoons cooking oil
2 medium carrots, thinly
*   sliced*
1 medium green pepper,
*   chopped (optional)*
16-ounce package Tinkyada[R]
*   Spaghetti Noodles*
3 green onions, sliced
1 tablespoon cornstarch
⅓ cup gluten-free soy sauce
1 tablespoon cooking oil

1. Drain pineapple, reserving ⅓ cup juice. Set aside.

2. Cook chicken, garlic, and ginger in oil until chicken begins to brown. Add carrots and green pepper. Cover and cook until vegetables and chicken are done.

3. While vegetables cook, boil spaghetti. Drain.

4. Add noodles and green onions to chicken mixture.

5. Combine cornstarch, soy sauce, and pineapple juice with 1 tablespoon oil. Stir into chicken and noodle mixture. Cook for 2 minutes or until sauce is thickened. Add pineapple and additonal soy sauce to taste..

Serves 6 to 8

Barbequed Chicken

4 to 5 boneless, skinless
*   chicken breasts*
1½ tablespoons gluten-free
*   Worcestershire sauce*
¾ cup grape jelly
1½ cups ketchup
3 tablespoons mustard
1 clove garlic, minced

1. Preheat oven to 350°F.

2. Place chicken breasts in a 9 x 13-inch greased casserole dish.

3. Combine ingredients for sauce and pour over chicken. Cover and bake chicken for 1 hour.

Serves 4 to 5

Chicken Strips

4 boneless, skinless chicken
    breasts, sliced in thin
    strips
¼ cup cornstarch
2 tablespoons corn flour
1 tablespoon brown rice
    flour
2 tablespoons cooking oil
garlic salt, to taste
onion salt, to taste
lemon pepper, to taste

1. Place cornstarch, corn flour, and brown rice flour in a plastic bag and mix. Add chicken strips and shake to cover chicken.

2. Coat the bottom of a nonstick frying pan with cooking oil. Fry chicken on both sides until browned and cooked. Add more oil, as needed.

3. Add garlic salt, onion salt, and lemon pepper, to taste.

Serves 4 to 5

Hot and Spicy Chicken

4 boneless, skinless chicken
    breasts, sliced in thin
    strips
¼ cup cornstarch
2 tablespoons corn flour
2 to 2¼ cups brown sugar
½ cup Frank's® Original Red
    Hot® Sauce
cooking oil

1. Mix cornstarch and corn flour in a plastic bag. Add chicken strips and shake until chicken is coated.

2. Coat the bottom of a nonstick frying pan with cooking oil. Brown chicken until cooked.

3. Combine brown sugar and hot sauce in a glass measuring cup. Microwave for 2 minutes, or until sugar is dissolved.

4. Add sauce to chicken and cook over medium heat for several minutes.

Serves 4 to 5

Chinese Noodles

4 bone-in chicken breasts
2 tablespoons chopped onion
or green onions
6 hard-boiled eggs
1 package Tinkyada Spaghetti
Noodles, cooked and
drained
garlic salt, to taste
onion salt, to taste
black pepper or lemon
pepper, to taste
gluten-free soy sauce, to taste

1. Place chicken breasts and seasonings in large pot. Add enough water to cover chicken. Cook until chicken is tender, approximately 2 to 3 hours for thawed, bone-in chicken. Remove chicken from pan, reserving broth. Allow chicken to cool slightly, then cut or tear into small pieces.

2. Combine chicken, onion, eggs, noodles, broth, and seasonings. Add soy sauce to taste. Serve in individual soup bowls.

Serves 6 to 8

Italian Chicken

4 boneless, skinless chicken
breasts
1 cup gluten-free spaghetti sauce
1 cup grated mozzarella cheese
garlic salt, to taste
3 tablespoons cooked,
crumbled bacon

1. Preheat oven to 350°F.

2. Place chicken breasts in a 9 x 13-inch casserole dish. Cover with spaghetti sauce, grated cheese, and bacon. Bake for 1 hour. Add garlic salt, to taste.

Serves 4

Lemon Basil Chicken

2 cups cooked, diced chicken
¼ cup cooked, crumbled
    bacon
1 tablespoon butter
1 cup water
¼ cup cornstarch
2 teaspoons crushed garlic
1 teaspoon dried basil
2 cups heavy whipping cream
2 teaspoons gluten-free beef
    bouillon
⅛ cup lemon juice
5 large mushrooms, sliced
1 cup artichoke hearts,
    drained
¼ cup sun-dried tomatoes
garlic salt, to taste
gluten-free spiral noodles,
    boiled and drained
Parmesan cheese, shredded

1. In a measuring cup, combine water with cornstarch.
2. Melt butter in frying pan. Add crushed garlic, basil, cream, beef bouillon, lemon juice, mushrooms, artichoke hearts, sun-dried tomatoes, and cornstarch mixture. Heat through, but do not boil.
3. Add chicken, bacon, and garlic salt.
4. Serve over noodles and top with freshly shredded Parmesan cheese.

Serves 5 to 7

Sweet and Sour Chicken

¾ cup sugar
¼ cup pineapple juice
½ cup apple cider vinegar
3 tablespoons ketchup
1 tablespoon gluten-free soy
   sauce
½ teaspoon salt
4 to 5 boneless, skinless
   chicken breasts,
    cut in strips
¼ cup cornstarch
cooking oil

1. In a saucepan, combine sugar, pineapple juice, cider vinegar, ketchup, soy sauce, and salt. Simmer over medium heat.

2. Meanwhile, dip chicken in cornstarch or shake the chicken with cornstarch in a ziptop plastic bag. Fry the chicken in cooking oil until browned and cooked through.

3. Pour heated sauce over chicken and heat until sauce is slightly thickened. Alternately, chicken can be fried until browned, placed in a casserole dish, covered with sauce, and baked at 350°F for 50 to 60 minutes.

Serves 4 to 6

Salt and Vinegar Chicken

8 chicken thighs or
   drumsticks (no boneless,
   skinless pieces)
1 cup apple cider vinegar
2 tablespoons salt
cooking oil

1. Preheat oven to 425°F.

2. Place the vinegar in a ziptop plastic bag. Add salt and close the bag. Squeeze and shake the bag until the salt dissolves in the vinegar.

3. Place the pieces of chicken in the bag with the salt–vinegar solution and squeeze and shake the mixture over the chicken.

4. Place the chicken in a casserole dish or metal cake pan that has been lined with aluminum foil and then covered with cooking oil. Bake for 1 hour

or more, uncovered. (This method will produce chicken with delicious, salty, crisp skin, but the oil will splatter in your oven. To ensure a clean oven, place the chicken in a plastic oven bag before baking. The skin won't be crispy, however.)

Serves 6 to 8

Baked Chicken

1 whole chicken*
water
garlic salt
onion salt

1. Preheat oven to 425°F.

2. Place chicken in a glass baking dish. Add water to barely cover the bottom of the dish. Sprinkle garlic salt and onion salt on top of the chicken. Bake uncovered at 425°F for ½ hour.

3. Cover chicken with foil and turn down to 350ºF. Bake for 1 hour, or until chicken is cooked. To determine if chicken is cooked, insert a fork or sharp knife into the thickest part of the chicken to see if juices run clear.

Serves 5 to 7

*Check to make sure that no broth with wheat in it has been injected into the chicken. Also, check the ingredients if the chicken has seasoning on it.

Tip: Chicken may also be placed in an oven bag before baking, with water or broth added to the bag.

Quick Chicken Tortillas

2 corn tortillas for each
serving
cooked, cubed chicken
cooked, crumbled bacon
grated cheese
diced onions
chopped cilantro (without
stems)
canned green chilies,
drained
diced tomatoes
fresh or canned salsa
sour cream

1. Butter one side of one tortilla per serving. Put butter side down in a nonstick frying pan.

2. Cover the tortilla with small portions of chicken, bacon, cheese, cilantro, and green chilies.

3. Butter one side of a second tortilla and place it, butter side up, on the covered tortilla in the pan. Lightly brown the bottom tortilla over medium heat until cheese melts. Turn over tortilla stack and brown the second buttered tortilla.

4. Serve with tomatoes, salsa, and sour cream.

Tip: Warming the tortillas in the microwave keeps them from breaking up. This will help the butter to spread more easily.

Barbecued Chicken with Smoked Sausage

1 bottle gluten-free honey
barbeque sauce
½ cup ketchup
2½ tablespoons gluten-free
Worcestershire sauce
⅔ cup brown sugar
½ cup diced onion
1½ tablespoons butter

1. Combine barbeque sauce, ketchup, Worcestershire sauce, and brown sugar in a medium bowl.

2. In a large frying pan, dice onion and sauté in butter until tender. Add sauce and sausage. Simmer for 2 hours.

3. Pour simmered sauce over prepared Chicken Strips and serve.

*1 cup sliced gluten-free
    smoked sausage*
*6 or 7 cooked, boneless,
    skinless chicken breasts
    prepared as chicken
    strips (see page 99)*

Serves 6 to 8

Honey Garlic Chicken

*4 boneless, skinless chicken
    breasts*
cooking oil
2 teaspoons minced garlic
¼ teaspoon salt
*1 tablespoon apple cider
    vinegar*
2 tablespoons butter
½ cup honey

Optional Ingredients for Wraps

gluten-free corn tortillas
cooked rice
ranch dressing
diced tomatoes
diced avocados

1. Slice chicken breasts into strips and cook in oil.

2. Place garlic, salt, vinegar, butter, and honey in a glass measuring cup or small bowl. Microwave until combined and pourable.

3. Pour sauce over chicken and fry for several more minutes. Serve chicken or make a wrap using a corn tortilla topped with cooked chicken, rice, ranch dressing, tomatoes, and avocados.

Serves 4 (or 6 to 8 wraps)

Chicken Fettuccine

8-ounce package cream
    cheese
¼ cup butter
½ cup Parmesan cheese
1½ cups milk
½ teaspoon garlic powder
¼ teaspoon pepper
¼ teaspoon minced garlic
1 cup sliced fresh
    mushrooms
1 tablespoon butter
5 slices bacon, cut into
    small pieces and
    cooked
1 to 2 cooked chicken
    breasts, diced
14-ounce package gluten-
    free fettuccine noodles,
    cooked and drained

1. In a saucepan, heat cream cheese, butter, Parmesan cheese, milk, garlic powder, and pepper until smooth and warm. Set aside to cool and thicken.

2. Sauté garlic and mushrooms in butter.

3. Gently combine sauce, mushrooms, bacon, and chicken with the cooked noodles.

Serves 7 to 9

Paprika Chicken

½ cup butter
½ cup brown rice flour
3¾ cups milk
1 tablespoon gluten-free
  chicken bouillon
1 teaspoon paprika

1. Melt butter in saucepan and add brown rice flour.

2. Add milk, bouillon, and paprika and cook over medium-high heat until thickened. Remove from heat.

¾ *cup sour cream*

garlic salt, to taste

onion salt, to taste

2 boneless, skinless chicken breasts, cooked and diced

8 to 10 baked potatoes

3. Add sour cream, garlic salt, onion salt, and cooked chicken. Serve over baked potatoes.

Serves 8 to 10

Honey Mustard Chicken

4 boneless, skinless chicken breasts

¼ *cup cornstarch*

2 tablespoons corn flour

2 tablespoons cooking oil

garlic salt, to taste

onion salt, to taste

¼ *cup butter*

½ *cup honey*

¼ *cup mustard*

¼ *teaspoon curry powder*

¼ *teaspoon salt*

cooked rice or noodles

1. Partially thaw chicken breasts and slice into strips.

2. Place cornstarch and corn flour in a ziptop plastic bag and mix together. Place chicken in the bag and shake until chicken is coated.

3. Coat nonstick frying pan with cooking oil. Fry chicken until brown, crispy, and completely cooked. Add more oil as needed. Add garlic salt and onion salt.

4. In a saucepan, melt butter and honey over medium heat. Add mustard, curry powder, and salt. Pour over chicken and fry until sauce thickens slightly.

5. Serve with cooked rice or cooked noodles.

Serves 4

Parmesan Cheese Chicken

4 chicken breasts

1 egg, mixed well with 1 teaspoon water

½ cup gluten-free breadcrumbs, sprinkled lightly with poultry seasoning

¼ cup Parmesan cheese

⅛ teaspoon paprika

¼ teaspoon Italian seasoning

¼ teaspoon salt

¼ teaspoon pepper

sliced ham (optional)

sliced cheese (optional)

Sauce

½ teaspoon mustard

3 tablespoons mayonnaise

1. Preheat oven to 350°F.
2. Dip chicken in egg. Combine breadcrumbs, cheese, paprika, Italian seasoning, salt, and pepper in pie plate. Dip chicken in breadcrumb mixture.
3. Place chicken on greased cookie sheet. (For easy cleanup, place a piece of foil on cookie sheet and spray foil with cooking spray.) Bake for 50 to 60 minutes. To make chicken cordon bleu, cover cooked chicken with slices of ham and cheese, then bake for 2 to 3 minutes until cheese melts.
4. Mix mustard and mayonnaise in small serving bowl. Serve sauce with chicken.

Serves 4

Lemon Chicken

4 boneless, skinless chicken breasts, sliced in thin strips

¼ cup brown rice flour

2 tablespoons corn flour

2 tablespoons butter

cooking oil

garlic salt, to taste

1. Slice chicken into strips.
2. Place brown rice flour and corn flour in a ziptop plastic bag and mix. Place chicken in the bag and shake to cover chicken.
3. Coat the bottom of a nonstick frying pan with butter and add cooking oil. Brown the chicken until it is completely cooked. Add garlic salt.

Sauce

⅓ cup sugar

2 tablespoons fresh lemon juice

1 teaspoon cooking oil

½ teaspoon pepper

2 teaspoons cornstarch

¼ teaspoon minced garlic

*1 teaspoon gluten-free
    chicken bouillon*

Sour Sauce for Lemon Chicken

1 teaspoon dried oregano

*½ teaspoon gluten-free
    seasoned salt*

¼ teaspoon pepper

*1 teaspoon dried parsley
    (or 1 tablespoon fresh)*

¼ cup water

3 tablespoons lemon juice

1 teaspoon minced garlic

*1 teaspoon gluten-free
    chicken bouillon*

4. Meanwhile, combine sugar, lemon juice, oil, pepper, cornstarch, garlic, and chicken bouillon in a blender.

5. Pour sauce onto chicken and fry until sauce thickens. Serve.

6. If you like tart lemon chicken, add the alternate sour sauce to the cooked chicken strips. To make the sauce, combine all ingredients in a blender until smooth, then pour over cooked chicken.

Serves 4 to 6

Chicken and Rice with Sweet Lemon Sauce

*4 to 5 boneless, skinless
    chicken breasts*
¼ cup cornstarch
2 tablespoons corn flour
*2 tablespoons brown rice
    flour*
2 tablespoons cooking oil
garlic salt, to taste
onion salt, to taste
fried rice (see page 94)

Sauce

2 tablespoons cornstarch
½ cup sugar
*1 tablespoon brown rice
    flour*
⅛ teaspoon salt
3 tablespoons lemon juice
1½ cups water

1. Partially thaw chicken breasts and slice into strips.

2. Place cornstarch, corn flour, and brown rice flour in a ziptop plastic bag and mix together. Place chicken in the bag and shake until chicken is coated.

3. Coat the bottom of a nonstick frying pan with cooking oil. Fry chicken in oil until brown and crispy and completely cooked. Add more oil as needed. Add garlic salt and onion salt.

4. To make sauce, combine cornstarch, sugar, brown rice flour, and salt. Add lemon juice and water and whisk until combined. Boil for 1 minute or until thick and clear.

5. Pour sauce over prepared chicken and serve. Extra sauce is delicious served over the fried rice.

Serves 4 to 6

Creamy Romano Chicken

1½ cups cooked, cubed
    chicken,
⅛ cup cooked, crumbled
    bacon
2 tablespoons butter
½ cup sliced fresh
    mushrooms
¼ cup diced green onions
⅛ cup sun-dried tomatoes
½ cup artichoke hearts
3 cups heavy whipping
    cream
¼ cup whole milk
¾ cup freshly grated
    Parmesan cheese
½ to 1 tablespoon black
    pepper
¼ cup freshly grated
    Romano cheese
gluten-free spiral noodles,
    boiled and drained

1. Melt butter in frying pan. Sauté sliced mushrooms and green onions.

2. Add sun-dried tomatoes, artichokes, cream, milk, pepper, and Parmesan cheese. Heat through but do not boil.

3. Serve over gluten-free spiral noodles. Sprinkle with freshly grated Romano cheese.

Serves 7 to 9

Chicken or Shrimp Stir-Fry

*2 cups cooked, cubed
chicken and/or 1 to 1½
pounds cooked shrimp*
1 stalk celery, sliced
2 carrots, grated
1 cup chopped onion
1 cup chicken broth
*2 tablespoons plus 1
teaspoon cornstarch*
½ teaspoon minced garlic
½ teaspoon ground ginger
*2 tablespoons gluten-free
soy sauce*
1½ teaspoons sugar
1 cup sugar snap peas
*1 cup fresh, sliced
mushrooms*
*8-ounce can water chestnuts
(optional)*
cooked rice or noodles

1. In a nonstick frying pan, sauté celery, carrots, and onion in oil over medium heat until tender. Add cooked chicken and/or shrimp and reduce heat to warm.

2. Combine cornstarch and chicken broth in a small saucepan. Heat and stir until clear and smooth.

3. Add garlic, ginger, soy sauce, and sugar. Stir until dissolved. Pour over chicken or shrimp and vegetables. Stir in mushrooms, sugar snap peas, and water chestnuts.

4. Serve over rice or gluten-free noodles.

Serves 4 to 6

Hawaiian Haystacks

Chicken

2 to 4 bone-in chicken breasts
*1 small onion, sliced into
large pieces*

1. Place chicken in a large pot and cover it with water. Add onion, celery, chicken bouillon, salt, pepper, and garlic salt and simmer for 2 to 3 hours until the chicken is tender. Remove chicken when fully cooked and allow it to cool slightly.

2 stalks celery, sliced
1 teaspoon gluten-free
    chicken bouillon
1 teaspoon salt
1 teaspoon pepper
½ teaspoon garlic salt

Rice

½ cup white rice
½ cup brown rice
1 cup water
1 cup chicken broth
½ teaspoon salt
¼ teaspoon gluten-free
    chicken bouillon
⅛ cup butter

Gravy

reserved chicken broth
cornstarch
garlic salt, to taste
onion salt, to taste
gluten-free chicken bouillon
chicken, cooked and cubed

Toppings

2 tomatoes, diced
2 stalks celery, diced
1 small can crushed
    pineapple
½ cup coconut
1 cup grated cheese

2. Cut the chicken into cubes. Strain the chicken broth into a glass measuring cup and set aside for gravy. Discard onions and celery.

3. Preheat oven to 350°F after the chicken has been cooking for 1 hour.

4. Combine white rice, brown rice, water, chicken broth, salt, chicken bouillon and butter in a glass 8 x 8-inch baking dish. Cover with foil and bake for 45 to 50 minutes, or until liquid is absorbed.

5. Prepare the gravy while rice is baking. Measure out one cup of the reserved chicken broth per person into a saucepan.

6. In a bowl, mix 1 tablespoon of cornstarch in ⅛ cup of cold water for each cup of stock until it makes a smooth, thin paste.

7. Heat the broth in a saucepan and stir in the cornstarch paste. Boil gently until smooth, clear, and thickened. If more cornstarch is needed, dissolve additional cornstarch in cold water, adding 1 teaspoon of water at a time, as needed.

8. Taste gravy and add additional seasonings and chicken bouillon, if needed. Add cooked, diced chicken to gravy.

9. Put diced tomatoes, diced celery, crushed pineapple, coconut, and grated cheese in separate bowls. Each person will build his or her own "haystack," beginning with rice, chicken and gravy, and toppings.

Makes 1 serving per cup of broth

Chinese Sweet and Sour

cooked rice
*1 pound meat of your
    choice, cubed*
1 tablespoon olive oil
*½ cup chopped green
    peppers*
*20-ounce can pineapple
    tidbits, drained*
*11-ounce can mandarin
    oranges, drained
    (reserve ¼ cup juice)*
1 cup water
¼ cup honey
¼ cup sugar
½ cup ketchup
1 cup brown sugar
¼ cup vinegar
*1 tablespoon gluten-free soy
    sauce*
3 tablespoons cornstarch

1. Brown meat and add peppers the last 2 to 3 minutes of cooking.

2. Reserve juice from mandarin oranges. Add pineapple and mandarin oranges to meat. Cover and remove from heat.

3. Combine water, honey, sugar, ketchup, brown sugar, vinegar, and soy sauce in separate pan. Bring to a boil.

4. Mix cornstarch with the reserved orange juice and add to boiling liquid. Let boil on medium heat until thick, about 2 to 3 minutes.

5. Add to cooked meat mixture. Serve with cooked rice.

Serves 6 to 8

Thai Red Curry

3½ cups cooked rice
2 to 3 boneless, skinless
*   chicken breasts*
1 tablespoon cooking oil
1 onion, thinly sliced
4 garlic cloves, crushed
1 teaspoon ground ginger
2 carrots, sliced
1 green or red pepper, diced
14-ounce can coconut
*   milk, or 2 cups heavy*
*   whipping cream*
1 teaspoon Thai red curry
*   paste*
2 tablespoons gluten-free
*   soy sauce*
2 tablespoons sugar
garlic salt, to taste

1. Slice chicken into strips and sauté with onion, garlic, and ginger in cooking oil. Remove from frying pan and set aside.

2. Sauté carrots and peppers until tender. Stir in coconut milk (or cream), curry paste, soy sauce, sugar, and garlic salt. Add chicken and onion mixture and simmer 3 to 4 minutes.

3. Serve over cooked rice, or add rice to the Thai red curry until liquid is absorbed by the rice.

Serves 4 to 6

Japanese Style Chicken

3 large boneless, skinless
*   chicken breasts, sliced in*
*   thin strips*
cooking oil
¼ to ⅓ cup gluten-free soy
*   sauce*
¼ cup brown sugar

1. Brown the chicken in oil until nearly done.

2. Combine soy sauce, brown sugar, garlic, ginger, and sesame oil. Add to chicken and cook over medium heat until chicken is completely done. Serve with cooked rice.

½ teaspoon minced garlic
½ teaspoon ground ginger
¼ teaspoon toasted sesame oil
sesame seeds
cooked rice
corn tortillas (optional)

Variation: Chicken Wrap

Place a few pieces of chicken and a spoonful of cooked rice in a warm tortilla. (To warm tortillas, place them in a moist paper towel or wrap them in a clean dish towel, then microwave until tortillas are soft and pliable, approximately 45 seconds for 2 tortillas.)

Serves 3 to 5

Tip: This chicken is delicious when it is cooked on a grill. Marinate the chicken in the sauce for several hours before grilling.

Red Sauce Creamy Enchiladas

6 bone-in chicken breasts
½ teaspoon salt
1 teaspoon garlic salt
1 teaspoon lemon pepper
1 teaspoon gluten-free
*   chicken bouillon*
1 tablespoon minced, dried
*   onion*
beef enchilada sauce (see
*   page 138)*
3 cups grated cheese
1½ cups sliced black olives
2 cups shredded lettuce
12 gluten-free corn tortillas
salsa

1. Pour six cups of water into a large pot. Add uncooked chicken breasts and salt, garlic salt, lemon pepper, chicken bouillon, and dried onion. Simmer until chicken is fully cooked and tender, approximately 2 to 3 hours. Reserve 2 cups of strained broth from pot.

2. Remove cooked chicken from bones and slice into small pieces.

3. Prepare beef enchilada sauce. Set aside.

4. In a small bowl, combine cold water and cornstarch and stir until smooth. Pour reserved chicken broth into saucepan and add cornstarch–water mixture.

sour cream
creamy enchilada sauce

Creamy Enchilada Sauce

⅛ cup cornstarch
¼ cup cold water
2 cups reserved chicken broth
½ cup sour cream
4-ounce can diced green chilies

5. Place saucepan over medium-high heat and bring mixture to a boil until thickened. Remove saucepan from heat, add sour cream and green chilies. Set aside.

6. Preheat oven to 350°F.

7. Soften tortillas in cooking oil in a frying pan over medium-high heat (or microwave tortillas until soft and pliable). Allow tortillas to cool slightly.

8. Spray a 9 x 13-inch baking pan with cooking spray. Pour ¼ cup beef enchilada sauce and ¼ cup creamy enchilada sauce on bottom of baking pan and spread to coat.

9. Pour remaining beef enchilada sauce into a pie plate. Dip softened tortillas one at a time into sauce. Divide sliced chicken into 12 equal piles. Make a line of chicken on each of the 12 tortillas, then sprinkle with ¼ cup grated cheese and ⅛ cup sliced olives.

10. Fold the tortillas in half and place in baking dish, overlapping them. Cover folded tortillas with remaining creamy enchilada sauce and any remaining beef enchilada sauce. Cover baking dish with foil and bake for 25 to 30 minutes, or until bubbling.

11. Serve with salsa, shredded lettuce, chopped tomatoes, and sour cream.

Serves 6 to 8

Creamy Chicken Enchiladas

*4 boneless, skinless chicken
    breasts*
⅓ cup butter
⅓ cup rice flour
3 cups chicken broth
*1 teaspoon to 1½ tablespoons
    diced jalapeno pepper
    (optional)*
1½ cups sour cream
*12 to 14 gluten-free corn
    tortillas*
2 cups grated cheese

1. Preheat oven to 350°F.

2. Bake chicken for approximately 1 hour in a covered casserole dish, with enough water to just cover the bottom of the dish.

3. Cut cooked chicken into cubes and place in large bowl.

4. In a medium saucepan, melt the butter. Stir in rice flour. Gradually pour in chicken broth. Add jalapeno pepper, if desired. Bring to a boil until slightly thickened. Remove from heat and add sour cream. Mix sauce well with a whisk.

5. Pour ½ cup sauce in the bottom of a greased 9 x 13-inch casserole dish.

6. Pour 1 cup of remaining sauce into the bowl with the cubed chicken. Mix well.

7. Wrap the stack of tortillas in a moist paper towel or in a clean dish towel. Place them in the microwave until they are soft and pliable, approximately 2 minutes for 12 tortillas. Allow tortillas to cool slightly.

8. Cup a tortilla in your hand and place a spoonful of chicken and sauce mixture down the center. Roll the tortilla and repeat. Place enchiladas side by side in casserole dish.

9. Cover rolled tortillas with remaining sauce and grated cheese. Bake at 350°F for 30 minutes.

Serves 6 to 8

Irish Nachos

*1 package gluten-free
    French fries*
1 package bacon
2 cups grated cheese
⅓ cup sliced green onions
½ cup diced tomatoes
*ranch dressing or cottage
    cheese*

1. Bake French fries according to package directions.

2. Fry bacon until crisp. Cut into small pieces.

3. Place French fries on serving plate. Top with bacon, cheese, onions, tomatoes, and dressing or cottage cheese.

Serves 5 to 7

Parmesan Pork Chops

1 egg
1 tablespoon water
*¾ cup gluten-free
    breadcrumbs*
½ teaspoon Italian seasoning
½ teaspoon dried parsley
*¾ cup grated Parmesan
    cheese*
4 center-cut pork loin chops
cooking oil
salt and pepper, to taste

1. Whisk the egg and water in a pie plate to blend.

2. Place the gluten-free breadcrumbs in another pie plate and sprinkle with Italian seasoning, parsley, and Parmesan cheese. Mix well.

3. Generously season the pork chops with salt and pepper, dip them in the egg mixture, and then coat them with the breadcrumbs, patting to adhere.

4. Fry pork chops in oil until completely cooked. Season with salt and pepper, to taste.

Serves 2 to 4

Sweet and Sour Pork Ribs

*4 to 6 country-style
    (boneless) pork ribs*
*½ cup pineapple juice (from
    can of pineapple chunks)*
½ cup brown sugar
⅓ cup apple cider vinegar
*1 cup gluten-free chicken
    broth*
*2 teaspoons gluten-free soy
    sauce*
½ teaspoon salt
½ teaspoon garlic salt
2 tablespoons cornstarch
*½ medium-size onion, thinly
    sliced*
½ green bell pepper, diced
½ cup pineapple chunks

1. Preheat oven to 300°F.
2. Combine pineapple juice, brown sugar, vinegar, chicken broth, soy sauce, salt, garlic salt, and cornstarch.
3. Place meat in a glass casserole dish and pour sauce over the meat. Cover with foil and bake for 2 hours and 15 minutes.
4. Reduce oven temperature to 250°F. Place the onion, green pepper, and pineapple around the meat. Cover and bake for 1 hour and 15 minutes, or until meat is fork-tender.

Serves 3 to 5

Tip: Use a meat thermometer to test pork for doneness. The center of the meat should reach 160° F.

Easy Quiche

butter
*gluten-free hot cereal, such
    as Bob's Red Mill*ᴿ
    Mighty Tasty
6 eggs, beaten
1½ cups whipping cream
½ cup milk

1. Preheat oven to 350°F.
2. Spread a thin layer of butter on a round quiche pan or pie plate. Sprinkle heavily with gluten-free hot cereal.
3. Mix eggs, cream, and milk. Pour onto cereal base.
4. To make quiche Lorraine or zucchini quiche, add extra ingredients to the mixture on crust.

Quiche Lorraine

*1¼ cups Swiss or Monterey
    Jack cheese*
*10 slices cooked bacon or ¼
    cup cooked bacon pieces*
dash of nutmeg

Zucchini Quiche

½ cup shredded zucchini
1¼ cups shredded cheese
2 garlic cloves, minced
¼ teaspoon onion powder

5. Bake quiche on lower rack of oven for 55 to 65 minutes or until filling is slightly puffed and lightly browned on top.

Serves 6 to 8

Tip: Be sure to cook the quiche long enough that the gluten-free cereal softens; otherwise, it will be crunchy.

Seasoned Pork Chops

4 to 6 pork chops
*3 tablespoons brown rice
    flour*
1½ teaspoons dried oregano
1 teaspoon salt
¼ teaspoon pepper
¼ teaspoon garlic powder
2 tablespoons oil
*20-ounce can pineapple
    chunks, undrained*
¼ cup water
2 tablespoons brown sugar
*2 tablespoons dried minced
    onion*
2 tablespoons ketchup

1. In a pie plate, combine brown rice flour, oregano, salt, pepper, and garlic powder. Dip both sides of pork chops in mixture.

2. Pour oil into a large frying pan or skillet. Place pork chops in pan and fry until browned.

3. Preheat oven to 350°F.

4. Combine pineapple, water, brown sugar, onion, and ketchup in a saucepan and heat until brown sugar dissolves.

5. Transfer pork chops to a 9 x 13-inch casserole dish and add sauce and pineapple. (Or serve pineapple separately instead of heating it.) Bake for 1 to 1½ hours.

Serves 4 to 6

Sweet and Sour Pork

4 boneless pork chops
⅓ cup cornstarch
garlic powder
1 cup sugar
½ cup apple cider vinegar
1 cup chicken broth (or 1
*   cup water mixed with 1*
*   teaspoon gluten-free*
*   chicken bouillon)*
⅓ cup ketchup
1½ tablespoons gluten-free
*   soy sauce*
fried rice (see page 94)

1. Preheat oven to 325°F.
2. Slice pork into cubes. Roll cubes in cornstarch. Place in nonstick skillet and sprinkle with garlic powder. Brown lightly on both sides.
3. Combine sugar, vinegar, chicken broth, ketchup, and soy sauce in a saucepan. Boil for 2 minutes.
4. Place pork in a 9 x 13-inch baking dish that has been sprayed with cooking spray. Pour sauce over pork and bake uncovered for 1 to 1½ hours or until pork is cooked through and tender. After 40 to 45 minutes of baking, check to ensure there is enough liquid and that the sauce is not burning. If needed, add a small amount of chicken broth to sauce to prevent burning.
5. Serve with prepared rice.

Serves 4 to 6

Pork Roast

1 pork roast (3 to 4 pounds
*   for a small roast, 5 to 6*
*   pounds for a large roast)*
cooking oil
salt and pepper, to taste
garlic salt, to taste

1. Preheat oven to 325°F.
2. Brown the roast in a deep, heavy pan with enough oil to cover the bottom.
3. Open the baking bag and place in a 9 x 13-inch casserole dish.

*1 tablespoon minced dried
    onion, or 1 small onion,
    sliced*
1 regular-size oven bag

4. Sprinkle roast with seasonings and top with onions. Place roast in baking bag.

5. Pour water (2 cups for a small roast, 4 cups for a large roast) in the pan used to brown the roast. Stir to make a broth from the meat juices.

6. Add broth to the seasoned roast inside of the baking bag. Close the bag with the tie provided and make 3 to 4 small slits in the top of the bag.

7. Bake for 3 to 4 hours or more, depending on the size and cut of the roast.

Serves 6 to 9

Old-Fashioned Milk Gravy

meat of choice
½ cup milk, per serving
*2 teaspoons cornstarch, per
    serving*
*¼ teaspoon salt and ⅛
    teaspoon pepper for each
    ½ cup milk*
*gluten-free chicken or beef
    bouillon powder, to taste*

1. Pan-fry beef sirloin tip steaks, cube steaks, pork chops, or pork cutlets in a heavy frying pan. Season with salt and pepper.

2. Remove cooked meat from the frying pan and skim off excess fat.

3. Using a wire whisk or mixing spring, combine milk, cornstarch, salt, and pepper in a small bowl. Stir milk mixture into meat drippings in frying pan.

4. Stir constantly while cooking on medium heat until thickened. Add additional milk or thickening, if needed, for desired consistency. Season gravy to taste with bouillon powder.

Easy Vegetable Noodle Casserole

7 link sausages (or 1 cup
cooked ground sausage)
1 bag frozen vegetables, or 3
to 4 cups fresh vegetables
1 package Thai Kitchen[R]
Instant Noodle Soup—
Spring Onion flavor
¾ cup grated cheese

1. Preheat oven to 350°F.

2. Cook and dice sausage.*

3. Steam vegetables until tender.

4. Bring water to a boil in a small saucepan. Add noodles and oil from packet, but do not add seasoning packet. Drain noodles and add seasoning packet. Stir well.

5. Combine cooked sausage, steamed vegetables, cooked noodles, and ½ cup grated cheese.

6. Place mixture in casserole dish and sprinkle top with remaining ¼ cup cheese. Warm casserole in oven until cheese is melted.

Serves 2 to 4

*To eliminate some of the fat from link sausage, place the sausage links in a skillet and add ½ cup water. Cover and cook for 5 minutes. Remove the lid and drain the grease. Cook approximately 12 to 15 minutes, turning with tongs until all sides are brown. Cut links into small pieces for the vegetable casserole. Kitchen scissors work well.

Tip: Six cooked shrimp, sautéed in butter and minced garlic, or two cups cooked chicken, are also very good in this recipe.

Sweet Pear Pork Chops

5 to 6 thin pork chops
3 tablespoons brown rice
*   flour*
1½ teaspoons dried oregano
1 teaspoon salt
¼ teaspoon pepper
¼ teaspoon garlic powder
cooking oil
1 cup pear juice
⅓ cup water
2 tablespoons brown sugar
1 tablespoon plus 1 teaspoon
*   cornstarch*

1. Trim excess fat from meat.

2. In a shallow dish, mix brown rice flour, oregano, salt, pepper, and garlic powder. Coat the pork chops on both sides using all of the mixture.

3. In a skillet, fry chops on both sides in cooking oil until completely cooked. Or place pork chops to 9 x 13-inch casserole dish with ½ cup water, and bake at 325°F for 1 to 1½ hours, or until fully cooked.

4. Remove pork chops from skillet or casserole dish and place on a serving platter.

5. In skillet, combine pear juice, water, brown sugar, and cornstarch and bring to a boil until thickened. Pour over cooked pork chops.

Serves 5 to 6

Grilled Steak

2 tri-tip or top sirloin steaks
cooking oil
garlic salt
pepper

1. Pour a light coating of oil on steak and spread it around with a spoon. Flip steaks over and repeat. Sprinkle well with garlic salt and pepper.

2. Cook steak on grill using medium heat.

Serves 2

Magnificent Steak Burritos

2 large steaks
3 tablespoons butter
6 mushrooms, sliced
¾ cup diced green pepper
½ cup diced onion
garlic salt
½ cup butter
½ cup brown rice flour
12-ounce can evaporated milk
2 cups gluten-free beef broth
1½ cups sour cream
10 gluten-free corn tortillas
1 cup grated cheese
shredded lettuce
sour cream
salsa

1. Grill steaks, then slice into thin strips.

2. Preheat oven to 350°F.

3. Melt butter in a frying pan and add mushrooms, green pepper, and onion. Sauté until tender. Sprinkle with garlic salt.

4. In a medium saucepan, melt butter and add brown rice flour. Stir well and add evaporated milk and beef broth. Bring to a boil until sauce thickens slightly. Remove from heat and add 1½ cups sour cream.

5. Grease or spray a 9 x 13-inch casserole dish. Pour ½ cup sauce into casserole dish and spread to cover bottom of dish.

6. Warm corn tortillas in microwave between moistened paper towels until softened.

7. Divide steak and cooked mushrooms, peppers, and onions between ten tortillas. Save one cup of sauce to top burritos. Use remaining sauce to cover steak and vegetables.

8. Roll tortillas and place in casserole dish. Pour reserved cup of sauce over burritos. Sprinkle with grated cheese. Bake for 25 to 30 minutes, or until cheese melts. Serve with shredded lettuce, a dollop of sour cream, and salsa.

Serves 5 to 7

Steak or Chicken Fajitas

3 medium-sized steaks (or 4
   boneless chicken breasts)

Marinade

2 tablespoons lime juice
2 tablespoons cooking oil
½ cup fresh cilantro, chopped
¼ cup gluten-free soy sauce
1 teaspoon gluten-free
   Worcestershire sauce
4 cloves minced garlic
1 teaspoon dried oregano
   leaves
½ teaspoon cumin

Vegetables

½ green bell pepper, sliced
½ red bell pepper, sliced
½ yellow bell pepper, sliced
½ large onion, sliced
6 to 8 corn tortillas
refried beans
chopped tomatoes
chopped cilantro
salsa
guacamole
sour cream

1. Slice steak (or chicken) into thin strips.

2. Pour marinade over strips of meat and marinate overnight in covered bowl or sealable bag.

3. Remove meat to a separate bowl, reserving marinade.

4. Pour enough of the reserved marinade in a nonstick pan to cover the bottom. Add vegetables and cook over medium heat until tender-crisp. Remove to platter and keep warm.

5. Add marinade to cover bottom of frying pan and add beef or chicken strips. Stir-fry meat until done.

6. Combine cooked vegetables and meat. Serve with warm tortillas, refried beans, chopped tomatoes, chopped cilantro, salsa, guacamole, and sour cream.

Serve 5 to 7

Guacamole

1 large avocado, mashed
½ cup gluten-free
*   mayonnaise*
¼ teaspoon lemon juice
3 tablespoons salsa
garlic salt, to taste

Peel avocado and remove pit. Mash with fork and add remaining ingredients. Stir well.

Tip: This guacamole is wonderful as a dip for potato chips.

Baked Potato Bar

6 baking potatoes
1 pound ground beef or
*   ground turkey*
½ cup chopped onion
4 fresh mushrooms, sliced
½ bag frozen broccoli
½ cup grated cheese
3 tablespoons bacon pieces
1 tomato, diced
ranch dressing, sour cream,
*   or cottage cheese*

1. Preheat oven to 400°F.
2. Scrub potatoes well, prick with a fork, and bake for 1 hour to 1¼ hours.
3. In a frying pan, brown ground meat and chopped onion. (If you are using ground turkey, you will need a small amount of oil for frying.)
4. Cook sliced mushrooms. Steam broccoli.
5. Put beef or turkey, onions, mushrooms, broccoli, bacon pieces, diced tomatoes, and ranch dressing, sour cream, or cottage cheese in individual bowls for self-serve.

Serves 5 to 6

Tip: If you wrap potatoes in aluminum foil for baking, wash them early so that they will be dry when wrapped in the foil. This prevents them from steaming.

Baked Potatoes with Chili Topping

6 baked potatoes
1 pound turkey burger
¼ cup diced green pepper
28-ounce can diced
    tomatoes, undrained
15-ounce can pinto beans
¼ teaspoon garlic powder
sprinkle of cayenne
    pepper
1 teaspoon cumin
½ teaspoon dried oregano
½ teaspoon pepper
½ teaspoon salt

1. Preheat oven to 400°F.
2. Scrub potatoes well, prick with a fork, and bake for 1 hour to 1¼ hours.
3. Brown the turkey burger and green pepper in oil.
4. Add tomatoes, pinto beans, garlic powder, cayenne pepper, cumin, oregano, pepper, and salt. Bring to a boil and reduce heat. Simmer for 30 minutes, stirring often.
5. Spoon topping onto baked potatoes.

Serves 5 to 6

Shepherd's Pie

1½ pounds ground beef or
    turkey burger
garlic salt, to taste
3 tablespoons cooking oil
½ cup chopped onion
¼ teaspoon salt
⅛ teaspoon pepper
two 15-ounce cans green
    beans, drained
two 8-ounce cans tomato
    sauce
2 cups mashed potatoes
grated cheese

1. Cook hamburger (or turkey burger and oil), pepper, and onion. Add green beans and tomato sauce.
2. Place in a 9 x 13-inch casserole dish with mashed potatoes and cheese on top. Bake at 350°F for 30 minutes, or until cheese melts.

Serves 6 to 8

Roast Beef

*1 cross-rib roast, chuck
    roast, or sirloin-tip roast*
*3 to 4 pounds for a small
    roast, 5 to 6 pounds for a
    large roast*
*1 tablespoon minced dried
    onion, or 1 small onion,
    sliced*
1 regular-size oven bag
cooking oil
salt
pepper
garlic salt

1. Preheat oven to 325°F.

2. Brown the roast in a deep, heavy pan with enough oil to cover the bottom of the pan.

3. Open baking bag and place it in a 9 x 13-inch casserole dish. Place roast in baking bag. Sprinkle the roast with seasonings and top with onions.

4. Pour water (2 cups for a small roast, 4 cups for a large roast) in the deep, heavy pan used to brown the roast. Stir to make a broth with the juices of the meat.

5. Add broth to the seasoned roast inside of the baking bag. Close the baking bag with the tie provided and snip 3 to 4 small slits in the top of the bag.

6. Bake roast for 3 to 5 hours, depending on the size and cut of the roast.

Serves 5 to 8

Gravy for Beef or Pork Roast

4 cups broth
4 tablespoons cornstarch
*6 tablespoons cold water
    or milk*
salt and pepper, to taste

1. To use broth from cooked roast, remove roast from baking bag and place on an oven-proof plate. Keep roast warm in oven.

2. Measure broth, then pour it through a strainer into a saucepan.

lemon pepper, to taste
garlic salt, to taste

3. Combine cornstarch and cold water or milk. Add cornstarch mixture to broth and cook over medium-high heat until it thickens. Add additional water if necessary.

4. Season gravy to taste with seasonings.

Slow-Cooked Roast

1 cross-rib or chuck roast
1 tablespoon gluten-free
   Worcestershire sauce
1 teaspoon crushed garlic

Gluten-free substitute for onion soup mix

1 tablespoon gluten-free
   beef bouillon
2 tablespoons dried minced
   onion
½ teaspoon onion powder
substitute for 1 can of cream
   of mushroom soup (see
   Mix for Easy Cream
   Soup, page 64)*

1. Preheat oven to 250°F.

2. Cover the bottom and sides of a 9 x 13-inch casserole dish with a piece of aluminum foil. Place roast on foil.

3. Mix remaining ingredients and pour over roast. Cover roast with a piece of aluminum foil. Fold over edges of the two pieces of foil together and seal. Bake roast for 8 to 9 hours. Use broth mixture for gravy.

Serves 5 to 8
*Most cream of mushroom or chicken soup has wheat in it.

Ground Beef Gravy with Potatoes

6 to 7 baked potatoes
1 pound ground beef
1 teaspoon crushed garlic
3 cups water
1 tablespoon gluten-free
    beef bouillon
3 tablespoons cornstarch

1. Brown the ground beef until cooked through. Move ground beef to a bowl, leaving bits of meat in the frying pan.

2. Combine garlic, water, bouillon, and cornstarch in a bowl. Mix well. Add to frying pan and bring to a boil. Stir constantly and reduce heat to medium. Cook until thickened.

Serves 5 to 7

Easy Chili

two 14.5-ounce cans stewed
    tomatoes, puréed in
    blender
two 15-ounce cans gluten-
    free chili
1 pound ground beef, cooked
1 onion, diced
15-ounce can kidney beans,
    drained
15-ounce can black beans,
    drained
1 teaspoon crushed garlic
chili powder to taste

1. Combine all ingredients.

2. Simmer in slow cooker on LOW for 6 to 8 hours.

Serves 7 to 9

Prize-Winning Chili

2 pounds extra lean ground beef
1 onion, sliced
four 16-ounce cans gluten-
    free pork and beans
15-ounce can pinto beans
15-ounce can kidney beans
14.5-ounce can diced tomatoes
1½ tablespoons chili powder
2 cups salsa
garlic salt, to taste
pepper, to taste

1. Fry ground beef and onion until completely cooked.

2. Drain and rinse pinto beans and kidney beans.

3. Combine all ingredients in a large pot. Bring to a gentle boil, then turn heat down and allow chili to simmer for 1½ hours, stirring occasionally.

Serves 8 to 10

Chili Relleno Casserole

two 4-ounce cans whole
    green chilies, drained
8 ounces Monterey Jack
    cheese, sliced in strips
4 eggs
1½ tablespoons milk
3½ tablespoons rice flour
¼ teaspoon salt
¼ teaspoon minced garlic
1 cup grated cheddar cheese

1. Preheat oven to 350°F.

2. Cut the green chilies in half lengthwise so you can lay them out flat. Place them in a single layer in a greased 9 x 13-inch baking dish and cover with cheese strips.

3. Separate the egg whites and yolks into two mixing bowls. Whip egg whites first at high speed until stiff peaks form.

4. Add milk, rice flour, salt, and garlic to the egg yolks and beat until smooth.

5. Fold egg-yolk mixture into beaten egg whites and spread over the chilies. Quickly top with grated cheddar cheese and bake for 16 to 20 minutes.

Serves 6 to 8

Bacon Ranch Hamburgers

4 hamburger patties
4 Kinnikinnick® gluten-free
    hamburger buns (or
    gluten-free bread)
8 slices bacon
1 large tomato, sliced
4 lettuce leaves
ranch dressing

1. Fry or grill hamburger patties. Fry bacon.

2. Microwave or toast gluten-free hamburger buns.

3. Serve hamburgers topped with 2 slices of bacon, tomato, lettuce, and ranch dressing.

Serves 4

Lasagna

10-ounce package gluten-
    free lasagna noodles
1 teaspoon minced garlic
1 pound ground beef
3½ cups gluten-free
    spaghetti sauce
½ cup water
1¾ cups cottage cheese
2 cups grated Italian blend
    cheese
¼ cup sour cream
grated Parmesan cheese

1. Preheat oven to 350°F.

2. Brown ground beef and add crushed garlic, spaghetti sauce, and water. Simmer for 4 to 5 minutes.

3. Spread a small amount of the sauce mixture in the bottom of a 9 x 13-inch baking dish. Place ⅓ of uncooked noodles on the sauce.

4. Combine cottage cheese, 1 cup of the grated cheese, and sour cream. Divide mixture in half and spread evenly over uncooked noodles. Top with another layer of noodles. Add half of remaining sauce and spread evenly over noodles.

5. Repeat with remainder of cottage cheese mixture and another layer of noodles. Add rest of sauce.

6. Top with reserved 1 cup of grated cheese. Sprinkle with Parmesan cheese. Cover lasagna and bake for 55 to 60 minutes, or until cheese melts and lasagna is heated through.

Serves 6 to 8

Barbecued Meatballs

Meatballs

1 pound ground beef
1 egg
1 small onion, diced
¾ cup gluten-free breadcrumbs
1 tablespoon gluten-free Worcestershire sauce
1 clove garlic, minced
1 teaspoon salt
½ teaspoon pepper

Barbecue Sauce

1½ tablespoons gluten-free Worcestershire sauce
¾ cup grape jelly
1½ cups ketchup
3 tablespoons mustard
1 clove garlic, minced

1. Preheat oven to 400°F.
2. Mix meatball ingredients and form into balls. Place in a 9 x 13-inch baking dish or jelly-roll pan. Pour barbecue sauce over meatballs. Bake uncovered for 20 to 25 minutes. Cooked meatballs should be firm.

Serves 5 to 7

Sweet and Sour Meatballs

Meatballs

1 pound ground beef
1 egg
1 small onion, diced
¾ cup gluten-free
*   breadcrumbs*
1 tablespoon gluten-free
*   Worcestershire sauce*
1 clove garlic, minced
1 teaspoon salt
½ teaspoon pepper

Sweet and Sour Sauce

1½ cups sugar
4 tablespoons cornstarch
4 tablespoons ketchup
1 tablespoon vinegar
1 cup pineapple juice
½ cup water
2 tablespoons lemon juice
cooked rice

1. Preheat oven to 400°F.

2. Mix meatball ingredients and form into balls. Place in 9 x 13-inch baking dish or jelly-roll pan and pour sweet and sour sauce over meatballs. Bake uncovered for 20 to 25 minutes. Cooked meatballs should be firm.

3. The sweet and sour sauce recipe makes a large amount of sauce, allowing for extra sauce to serve over rice as a side dish with the meatballs. If no extra sauce is needed, cut amounts in half. Combine sauce ingredients and boil until thick. Pour over meatballs and cooked rice.

Serves 5 to 7

Beef Stroganoff

Cooked gluten-free elbow
 or fettuccine noodles
 or rice
1 pound beef sirloin steak
 (or leftover roast beef)
1 tablespoon rice flour
½ teaspoon salt
2 tablespoons butter
1½ cups fresh mushrooms,
 sliced
½ cup diced onion
1 clove garlic, minced

Sauce

2 tablespoons butter
2 tablespoons rice flour
1 teaspoon gluten-free
 beef bouillon
¼ teaspoon salt
1¼ cups water
½ cup sour cream
1 tablespoon rice flour

1. Slice meat into thin strips while partially frozen, across the grain of the meat.

2. Combine rice flour and salt. Coat meat with mixture.

3. Heat butter in a skillet. Add meat and brown quickly on both sides.

4. Add mushrooms, onion, and garlic. Cook until onions are tender.

5. Remove meat–vegetable mixture from pan and set aside. Reserve drippings in pan.

6. To make sauce, add butter and rice flour to pan drippings in skillet and cook on medium-high heat. Add bouillon, salt, and water. Stir constantly with a whisk until mixture simmers and thickens.

7. Place meat mixture back in skillet. Combine sour cream and rice flour, then add to sauce mixture. Heat through but do not boil.

8. Serve over cooked gluten-free elbow or fettuccine noodles, or cooked rice.

Serves 5 to 7

Beef Enchiladas

1 pound ground beef
12 gluten-free corn
    tortillas
1 can refried beans
1 onion, chopped
gluten-free enchilada sauce
    (or use recipe below)
2 cups grated cheese
sour cream
shredded lettuce
chopped tomatoes

Beef Enchilada Sauce

2 cups water
⅛ cup cornstarch
½ tablespoon chili powder
1 teaspoon onion powder
½ teaspoon garlic powder
1 tablespoon gluten-free
    beef bouillon
⅛ teaspoon dried oregano
¼ cup cooking oil
¼ teaspoon salt
½ tablespoon sugar
¼ teaspoon cumin

1. Preheat oven to 350°F.

2. Brown ground beef.

3. Combine sauce ingredients and boil for 1 minute.

4. Microwave tortillas in slightly moist paper towels until pliable.

5. Mix refried beans and cooked ground beef in frying pan and warm through. Place beans and ground beef in tortilla and roll up.

6. Line up rolled tortillas in a greased 9 x 13-inch casserole dish. Cover tortillas with sauce and cheese. Bake for 35 to 45 minutes.

7. Top enchiladas with sour cream, lettuce, and tomatoes.

Serves 6 to 8

Green Chili Tacos

1 pound ground beef
1 teaspoon minced garlic
1 small onion, diced
4-ounce can diced green chilies
1 tomato, chopped
1¼ cups grated cheddar cheese
6 to 8 gluten-free taco shells
2 cups shredded lettuce
1 fresh tomato, chopped
1 small onion, diced
fresh or bottled salsa
ranch dressing

1. Brown the ground beef with garlic and onion. Drain off fat.

2. Add green chilies, tomato, and cheese. Heat through, stirring often.

3. Put meat mixture into hard taco shells or warmed corn tortillas and serve with lettuce, fresh chopped tomatoes, onions, salsa, and ranch dressing.

Serves 4 to 6

Beef or Chicken Tacos

1 pound cooked ground beef
*   or chicken*
gluten-free taco seasoning
*   mix or Mexican seasoning,*
*   to taste*
2 cups shredded lettuce
2 cups grated cheese
¼ cup diced onions
½ cup diced tomatoes
12 gluten-free corn tortillas
*   or corn shells*
sour cream or ranch dressing
salsa

1. Cook ground beef or chicken in a skillet. Sprinkle with taco seasoning mix or Mexican seasoning.

2. Prepare vegetables and other toppings.

3. Warm tortillas in a slightly moist paper towel (or clean dish towel) in the microwave until heated through and soft.

4. Serve tacos with gluten-free sour cream or ranch dressing and gluten-free salsa.

Serves 5 to 7

Meatloaf

1 pound ground beef
1 egg, slightly beaten
½ cup gluten-free
    breadcrumbs or
    cracker crumbs
½ cup diced onion
1 clove garlic, minced
1 tablespoon ketchup
1 tablespoon horseradish
1½ teaspoons salt
1 teaspoon sugar
⅓ cup milk

1. Preheat oven to 350°F.

2. Combine egg with ground beef. Add crumbs, onion, garlic, ketchup, horseradish, salt, sugar, and milk and mix well. Press into a loaf pan.

3. Spread additional ketchup on top, if desired. Cover with foil and bake for 1 hour.

Serves 5 to 7

Spaghetti

16-ounce package gluten-free
    spaghetti noodles
½ pound ground beef
3 cups gluten-free spaghetti
    sauce
1 teaspoon minced garlic
garlic salt, to taste
onion salt, to taste
¼ cup Parmesan cheese

1. Cook ground beef until browned. Combine with sauce, and season with garlic and onion salt. Simmer for at least 15 minutes.

2. While simmering meat and sauce, cook spaghetti noodles. Drain and rinse.

3. Serve with Parmesan cheese sprinkled on top.

Serves 8

Tip: Consider using this recipe as a side dish, with elbow or spiral noodles in place of the spaghetti noodles.

Roast Beef Wrap

1 cup cooked roast beef
2 cups gravy
*4-ounce can diced green
    chilies*
1 tablespoon sour cream
6 tortillas, warmed
grated cheese

1. Chop roast into small pieces.
2. Place meat, gravy, and green chilies in a frying pan and heat until warm.
3. Warm tortillas in the microwave, or fry them in hot oil until soft.
4. Make a line of meat–gravy mixture down the middle of each tortilla. Sprinkle with grated cheese. Roll tortillas and serve.

Serves 4 to 6

Sloppy Joe Wrap

1 pound ground beef
*½ cup chopped onion, or 1
    tablespoon minced dried
    onion*
¼ cup chopped celery
8-ounce can tomato sauce
*1½ teaspoons gluten-free
    Worcestershire sauce*
¼ cup ketchup
*1 teaspoon apple cider
    vinegar*
1 tablespoon brown sugar
½ teaspoon salt
½ teaspoon pepper
½ teaspoon minced garlic

1. Brown the ground beef with onions and celery.
2. Add remaining ingredients and simmer until vegetables are tender. Serve on warmed corn tortillas.

Serves 4 to 6

Tortilla Wrap Ideas

Wrap gluten-free corn tortillas in a moist paper towel or in a clean dish towel and place them in the microwave until they are soft and pliable, approximately 2 minutes for 12 tortillas. Tortillas may also be warmed by quickly frying them in hot oil.

Hard-Boiled Egg Wrap

Top a microwaved tortilla with hard-boiled eggs mixed with mayonnaise. Add lettuce and pickle relish or a dill pickle spear.

Lunch Meat Wrap

Top a microwaved tortilla with mayonnaise and a piece of gluten-free lunch meat. Add lettuce, chopped tomatoes, and a dill pickle spear.

Chicken Wrap

Top a microwaved tortilla with gluten-free chicken chunks mixed with mayonnaise. Add avocado spears, shredded lettuce, bacon pieces, and lemon pepper.

Chili Wrap

Top a fried or microwaved tortilla with gluten-free chili, shredded cheese, lettuce, and ranch dressing.

Pizza Tortillas

Top a tortilla with spaghetti sauce, pepperoni, cheese, and other desired toppings. Put another tortilla on top and fry in a small amount of oil on both sides until lightly browned and cheese is melted. Cut into pie-shaped pieces and serve warm.

Spanish Wrap

Top a fried or microwaved tortilla with a scoop of refried beans. Add lettuce, shredded cheese, chopped tomatoes, and a mixture of ranch dressing and salsa.

Tuna Wrap

Top a microwaved tortilla with mayonnaise and tuna, a pickle spear, and lettuce.

Scrambled Egg Wrap

Top a fried or microwaved tortilla with scrambled eggs, bacon pieces, mayonnaise, and shredded cheese.

Cinnamon Sugar Wrap

Spread a microwaved tortilla with butter and cinnamon sugar. Roll tortilla and slice it into 1-inch pieces. Secure with toothpick, if desired.

Alfredo Pizza

2 teaspoons yeast
½ cup lukewarm water
2 teaspoons sugar
1¼ cups warm milk
2 cups rice flour
1½ cups tapioca flour
2½ teaspoons xanthan gum
½ cup dried potato flakes
1 teaspoon salt
1½ teaspoons Italian seasoning
¼ cup shortening
2 tablespoons butter
4 ounces cream cheese
⅛ cup butter
¼ cup Parmesan cheese
¾ cup milk
¼ teaspoon garlic powder
¼ teaspoon pepper
5 pieces bacon, fried
2 chicken breasts
¼ teaspoon seasoned salt
1 cup grated cheese
Additional toppings
   could include artichoke
   hearts, green onions,
   fresh tomatoes, green
   peppers, and yellow
   summer squash

Prepare Alfredo sauce at least a half hour ahead to allow time for sauce to thicken before beginning pizza.

1. Combine cream cheese, butter, Parmesan cheese, milk, garlic powder, and pepper in medium saucepan and cook until smooth and warm. Refrigerate for ½ hour or more.

2. Preheat oven to 400°F.

3. Pour warm water into a small bowl, and sprinkle yeast and sugar on top of water.

4. Microwave milk until warm.

5. Combine rice flour, tapioca flour, xanthan gum, potato flakes, and seasoning in the bowl of a heavy-duty kitchen mixer.

6. Mix yeast mixture, warm milk, shortening, and butter into dry ingredients. Beat at high speed for 3 minutes.

7. Spray or grease 2 large pizza pans. Divide dough in half.

8. Place hands in plastic bags and press dough evenly onto pizza pans. Bake 10 minutes on middle shelf of oven.

9. Cut cooked bacon and chicken into small pieces. Add seasoned salt to chicken and stir well. Spread sauce over pizza crusts. Top with cooked bacon, cooked chicken, grated cheese, and desired additional toppings. Bake for approximately 10 minutes.

Serves 9 to 14

Pizza

2 teaspoons yeast
½ cup lukewarm water
2 teaspoons sugar
1¼ cups warm milk
2 cups rice flour
1½ cups tapioca flour
2½ teaspoons xanthan gum
½ cup dried potato flakes
1 teaspoon salt
1½ teaspoons Italian
*   seasoning*
¼ cup shortening
2 tablespoons butter
gluten-free spaghetti sauce
shredded cheese
toppings such as
*   pepperoni, Canadian*
*   bacon, mushrooms*
*   olives, green peppers*

1. Preheat oven to 400°F.

2. Pour warm water into a small bowl, and sprinkle yeast and sugar on top of water.

3. Microwave milk until warm.

4. Combine rice flour, tapioca flour, xanthan gum, potato flakes, and seasoning in the bowl of a heavy-duty kitchen mixer.

5. Mix yeast mixture, warm milk, shortening, and butter into dry ingredients. Beat at high speed for 3 minutes.

6. Spray or grease 2 large pizza pans. Divide dough in half.

7. Place hands in clean plastic bags and press dough evenly onto pizza pans. Bake 10 minutes on middle shelf of oven.

8. Add sauce, pepperoni, Canadian bacon, cheese (or non-dairy substitute), and additional toppings. Bake another 10 to 20 minutes until bottom of crust is lightly browned.

Serves 9 to 14

Rich and Cheesy Halibut

¼ cup grated Parmesan
    cheese
2 tablespoons butter,
    softened
2 teaspoons mayonnaise
2 teaspoons lemon juice
2 tablespoons chopped
    green onions
¼ teaspoon salt
4 halibut fillets

1. Preheat oven broiler. Grease a 9 x 13-inch baking dish.

2. In a small bowl, mix the Parmesan cheese, butter, mayonnaise, lemon juice, green onions, and salt. Arrange the halibut fillets in the prepared baking dish.

3. Broil the fillets for 8 to 10 minutes, or until easily flaked with a fork. Spread with the Parmesan cheese mixture and continue broiling for 2 minutes, or until topping is bubbly and lightly browned.

Serves 4

Marinated Italian Halibut

2 halibut fillets
¼ teaspoon dried thyme
½ teaspoon dried basil
¼ teaspoon onion powder
¼ teaspoon garlic powder
½ cup Italian dressing
garlic salt, to taste

1. Combine thyme, basil, onion powder, garlic powder, and Italian dressing. Marinate halibut in mixture for at least 2 hours.

2. Preheat grill and place halibut on the grill and sprinkle with garlic salt. Grill until fish flakes easily with a fork.

Serves 2

Flavorful Baked Fish

1 tablespoon butter

1 small onion, cut in
   quarters and thinly
   sliced

4 fresh or frozen cod,
   haddock, or halibut
   fillets, thawed*

1 teaspoon seasoned salt

1 teaspoon garlic salt

¼ teaspoon black pepper or
   lemon pepper

¼ cup grated Parmesan
   cheese

¼ cup mayonnaise

1 tablespoon fresh parsley
   or cilantro

1 tablespoon lemon juice or
   apple cider vinegar

¼ cup sliced almonds

1 tablespoon butter

1. Preheat oven to 400°F. Sauté the onion in butter in a small frying pan.

2. Spread onions in a 9 x 13-inch glass baking dish. Arrange the fish on the onion and sprinkle with seasoned salt, garlic salt, and pepper.

3. In a small bowl, combine Parmesan cheese, mayonnaise, parsley, and lemon juice. Spread on fish. Bake uncovered for 10 minutes.

4. While fish is baking, place almonds in small frying pan with 1 tablespoon of butter and stir until almomds just start to turn golden brown. Sprinkle almonds on fish and bake for an additional 10 minutes or until fish flakes easily with a fork.

Serves 4

*If using fresh trout, remove the skin before adding the topping. This can be done by baking the fish, covered with aluminum foil, for fifteen minutes. Let the fish cool enough to handle, and then pull the skin off. Put the sautéed onion, topping, and the almonds on the fish. Remove foil and bake until done. Baking times will vary with the size of the fillets or the fresh fish.

Fish Tacos with Sweet Cucumber Salsa

*4 pieces flounder, or 3
    pieces salmon*
¼ cup olive oil
½ cup sliced onion
1 tablespoon orange zest
juice from 2 oranges
*2 tablespoons chopped
    cilantro, stems removed*
1 teaspoon salt
¼ teaspoon black pepper
¼ teaspoon ground ginger
*2 cups finely shredded
    purple cabbage*
12 corn tortillas
cooking oil
*fresh shredded Parmesan
    cheese*
*gluten-free barbeque sauce
    (optional)*
*cilantro and lime wedges for
    garnishing, if desired*

Cilantro Dressing

*¼ cup thinly sliced green
    onions*
*¼ cup firmly packed cilantro
    leaves*

1. Combine olive oil, orange juice, orange zest, cilantro, salt, pepper, and ginger. Add fish and marinate at least 2 hours.

2. To make the dressing, place all ingredients in a blender and blend until smooth.

3. To make the salsa, combine ingredients in a small bowl and sit at room temperature for 30 minutes to let the flavors blend.

4. Preheat oven broiler.

5. Lightly spray oven broiler pan. Place marinated fish on baking sheet and season with additional salt and pepper. Broil about 6 to 8 minutes, or until fish is lightly browned on top and flakes easily with a fork.

6. Sauté onion and fry tortillas lightly in oil.

7. Assemble cooked fish, onion, cabbage, shredded Parmesan, barbeque sauce, cilantro dressing, and sweet cucumber salsa on a hot fried tortilla, then serve.

Serves 4 to 6

½ cup sour cream
½ cup mayonnaise
juice of 1 lime
½ teaspoon garlic powder
2 tablespoons grated
    Parmesan cheese
1 teaspoon sugar

Sweet Cucumber Salsa

1 cup crushed pineapple
1 cup diced cucumber
2 tablespoons chopped
    cilantro, stems removed
juice of 1 lime
4-ounce can chopped green
    chilies
garlic salt, to taste

Fried Fish

5 pieces snow cod or
    pollock
¼ cup brown rice flour
¼ cup corn flour
cooking oil
garlic salt, to taste
lemon pepper, to taste

1. Combine brown rice flour and corn flour in a pie plate. Dip fish on both sides in flour mixture.

2. Place fish in a nonstick frying pan or on a griddle coated with oil. Sprinkle both sides of fish with garlic salt and lemon pepper. Fry until golden brown and cooked throughout.

Serves 5

Grilled Salmon

2 teaspoons olive or cooking
   oil
2 teaspoons fresh lemon
   juice
½ teaspoon salt
2 garlic cloves, minced
   (about 1½ teaspoons)
1 teaspoon dried basil or
   thyme leaves
½ teaspoon lemon pepper
3 pieces salmon or about
   1 pound

1. Combine oil, lemon juice, salt garlic, basil or thyme, and lemon pepper in a large ziptop freezer bag. Squeeze bag until ingredients are mixed.

2. Add salmon and coat with mixture. Remove salmon and place on broiler pan sprayed with oil. Broil until salmon is cooked throughout, approximately 6 to 10 minutes. Or bake the salmon in sealed foil at 375°F for 35 to 45 minutes.

Serves 5 to 6

Desserts

Pretzel Cereal Snack

3 tablespoons honey

2 tablespoons butter

3 tablespoons peanut butter

2 cups Health Valley^R Rice
    Crunch 'Ems

2 cups EnviroKidz^R Gorilla
    Munch

1 package Ener-G^R Foods
    Crisp (gluten-free)
    Pretzels

⅓ cup peanuts (optional)

1. Preheat oven to 175°F.

2. Combine honey, butter, and peanut butter and heat in microwave for 1 minute or less, until mixture is smooth.

3. Pour over combined cereal, pretzels, and peanuts and mix well. Spread on baking sheet and bake for 1 to 1½ hours.

Serves 4 to 6

Coconut and Almond Cereal Bars

2 cubes butter

1½ cups light corn syrup

1½ cups sugar

12-ounce box Rice Chex^R or
    Health Valley^R Rice
    Crunch 'Ems

¾ teaspoon baking soda

2 teaspoons vanilla

½ cup coconut

1 cup almond slivers

1. Boil butter, corn syrup, and sugar until it reaches the soft-ball stage on a candy thermometer.

2. Remove from stove and add soda and vanilla. Mix well and add cereal, coconut, and almonds. Stir well.

3. Press into greased 9 x 13-inch casserole dish.

Serves 9 to 12

Peanut Butter Cereal Bars

1 cup corn syrup
1 cup sugar
1¼ cups creamy peanut
   butter
3 cups Post® *Cocoa Pebbles*
4½ cups Health Valley® *Rice*
   Crunch 'Ems

1. Heat corn syrup, sugar, and peanut butter and mix together until consistency is smooth and sugar dissolves.
2. Add cereal and stir well. Press into a greased 9 x 13-inch casserole dish.

Serves 9 to 12

Cornflake Treats

1 cup sugar
1 cup corn syrup
½ teaspoon salt
½ teaspoon vanilla
1 cup peanut butter
8 cups gluten-free cornflakes
   or EnviroKidz®
   Amazon Frosted Flakes

1. Stir and boil sugar and corn syrup until sugar is dissolved. Do not boil too long, or treat will be too firm.
2. Add salt, vanilla, peanut butter and cornflakes and stir well. Press into greased 9 x 13-inch casserole dish and wait until treats are firm before serving.

Serves 9 to 12

Rice-Cake Candy Bars

¼ cup honey or sugar

⅓ cup almond or peanut butter

1 tablespoon cocoa or carob powder

1 to 2 tablespoons very hot water

⅓ cup slivered almonds

⅓ cup sunflower seeds

1 cup brown rice cakes, broken into small pieces

1. Chop almonds and sunflower seeds in blender. Set aside.

2. Heat sugar and peanut butter. Add cocoa and hot water, then almonds and sunflower seeds. Take off heat and add broken rice cakes.

3. Form into bars on pieces of aluminum foil. Wrap up and refrigerate or freeze.

Serves 2 to 4

Marshmallow Treats

⅓ cup butter

½ package marshmallows (about 36 large)

6 to 6½ cups Post Cocoa Pebbles[R]*, Post Fruity Pebbles*[R]*, Health Valley Rice Crunch 'Ems*[R]*, or EnviroKidz*[TM]* Gorilla Munch Cereal, or a mixture of these*

1. Melt butter and marshmallows in a large saucepan over medium heat.

2. Add cereal and stir well. Press into a greased 9 x 13-inch casserole dish.

Serves 9 to 12

Caramel Corn

6 quarts popped popcorn
½ cup butter
¼ cup light corn syrup
1 cup brown sugar
½ teaspoon salt
½ teaspoon vanilla extract
½ teaspoon baking soda
    (optional)

1. Bring butter, corn syrup, brown sugar, and salt to a rolling boil for 1 minute. Remove from heat. Add vanilla extract. For crispy popcorn, add baking soda.

2. Pour over popcorn and stir.

3. For crispy popcorn, bake at 350°F for 2 to 5 minutes on a greased cooking sheet.

Serves 8 to 10

Hard Candy

2 cups sugar
1 cup water
⅔ cup corn syrup
1 teaspoon flavoring, such
    as cinnamon, root beer,
    or lemon extract

1. Boil first three ingredients for 25 to 30 minutes or until mixture reaches 300°F on a candy thermometer.

2. Add flavoring. Pour into a greased jelly-roll pan or candy molds. Use caution, as mixture will be extremely hot.

Serves 8 to 10

Peanut Butter Heaven

1 cup sugar
1 cup light corn syrup
1 cup peanut butter
4 cups gluten-free
    EnviroKidz™ Koala
    Crisp® Cereal
½ cup milk chocolate chips
½ cup butterscotch chips

1. Bring sugar and corn syrup to a boil. (Do not boil very long or dessert will harden too much.)

2. Add peanut butter and mix well. Add cereal and stir until combined.

3. Lightly grease a 9 x 13-inch casserole dish with cooking spray. Scoop mixture into dish and press down until mixture is level.

4. Melt chocolate and butterscotch chips in microwave, watching them carefully so they don't burn.

5. Spread over cereal mixture. Refrigerate until ready to serve.

Serves 9 to 12

Rice Pudding

1 tablespoon butter
4 cups half-and-half, soy
    milk, or almond milk
1¼ cups cooked rice
¼ teaspoon salt
½ cup honey
4 eggs, slightly beaten
¼ teaspoon vanilla
½ teaspoon lemon extract
nutmeg

1. Preheat oven to 300°F. Grease 1½-quart glass baking dish with butter.

2. Combine all ingredients except nutmeg and pour into baking dish. Sprinkle top of pudding with nutmeg.

3. Bake uncovered for 35 to 45 minutes. Pudding will start to gel when it is done. Turn oven off and leave pudding in oven for 10 minutes, then remove, cool slightly, and serve.

Serves 6 to 8

Corn Chip Candy

1 cup peanut butter
1 cup light corn syrup
¾ cup sugar
9.25-ounce package Fritos®

1. Pour corn chips into a large bowl.

2. Heat peanut butter, corn syrup, and sugar until it comes to a boil. Quickly remove from heat and pour over corn chips. Stir well.

Serves 8 to 10

Apple Crisp

2 quarts gluten-free apple
*   pie filling (see page 193)*
¾ cup brown sugar
¼ cup brown rice flour
¼ cup tapioca flour
½ cup crumbled salted rice
*   cakes, or gluten-free*
*   oatmeal**
¾ teaspoon cinnamon
⅓ cup soft butter

1. Preheat oven to 375°F.

2. Pour apple pie filling into a 9 x 13-inch casserole dish.

3. Combine sugar, rice flour, tapioca flour, rice cakes, and cinnamon in a medium bowl. Cut butter in. Sprinkle mixture over top of pie filling.

4. Bake for 40 to 45 minutes.

Serves 9 to 12

*Some people with celiac disease cannot tolerate gluten-free oatmeal. Please check with your physician before adding oatmeal to your diet.

Best Toffee

2⅓ cups chopped almonds

two 7-ounce grated
    chocolate bars

1 pound butter

2½ cups sugar

⅓ cup almonds

2 tablespoons light corn
    syrup

1 cup water

1. Divide almonds as follows: 1 cup for bottom of toffee, 1 cup for top of toffee, and ⅓ cup in toffee.

2. Grate one candy bar at a time and place shavings in two separate bowls.

3. Spread 1 cup almonds on cookie sheet, then sprinkle with shavings from one candy bar.

4. Combine butter, sugar, almonds, corn syrup, and water in heavy saucepan. Bring to a boil over medium-high heat, stirring constantly until mixture reaches 285°F and color changes to a medium tan.

5. Pour mixture onto almonds and chocolate. Pour from the center outward.

6. Sprinkle remaining almonds and chocolate over hot toffee and press them into toffee with a drinking glass.

7. Allow toffee to set up for 5 hours at room temperature. Do not cool toffee in fridge or freezer.

Serves 15 to 20

Tips

1. When cooking toffee, you can turn the heat up, but don't turn it down.

2. Leave a metal spoon with a heat-proof handle in the toffee. If you remove it, get another clean spoon. This reduces the chance of toffee forming sugar crystals.

Fudge

2 cups sugar
⅔ cup evaporated milk or
    soy milk
2 tablespoons butter
dash of salt
1½ cups milk chocolate
    chips
2½ cups miniature
    marshmallows
2 teaspoons vanilla

1. Combine sugar, evaporated milk, butter and salt and boil for 5 minutes in saucepan.

2. Remove from heat and add chocolate chips and marshmallows. Stir until chocolate and marshmallows are melted. Add vanilla and stir well.

3. Spray an 8 x 8-inch casserole or baking dish with cooking spray. Spread fudge into dish. Cool completely in fridge before serving.

Serves 9

Rocky Road Fudge

4½ cups sugar
1 can evaporated milk
2 cubes butter
2 cups milk chocolate chips
1 large bag miniature
    marshmallows
three 7-ounce milk chocolate
    bars, frozen
2 tablespoons vanilla

1. Place sugar, evaporated milk, and butter in a saucepan and bring to a boil. Reduce heat and cook mixture for 10 minutes.

2. Remove from heat and add chocolate chips, marshmallows, frozen chocolate bars, and vanilla. Stir until smooth. (Frozen candy bars should keep the marshmallows from melting, which produces the "rocky road" style of fudge.)

3. Spray a 9 x 13-inch casserole dish with cooking spray. Spread fudge into dish. Cool completely in fridge before serving.

Serves 12 to 15

Chocolate Surprise

1st Layer

*graham cracker crust
(see page 166)*

2nd Layer

*1 cup powdered sugar
8-ounce package cream
cheese
1 cup Cool Whip*[R] *topping
from 12-ounce container*

3rd Layer

*6-ounce box chocolate
pudding (not instant)
3.4-ounce box chocolate
pudding (not instant)
milk (see pudding directions)*

4th Layer

remainder of Cool Whip[R]

1. Make graham cracker crust according to recipe on page 166. Bake in a 9 x 13-inch casserole dish. Cool crust completely.

2. Cream together powdered sugar and cream cheese. Fold in Cool Whip[R] topping. Smooth mixture on top of crust and place in fridge while preparing next layer.

3. Prepare pudding according to package directions and allow to cool slightly. Pour over cream cheese layer.

4. When pudding has completely cooled, add rest of Cool Whip[R] topping by the spoonful and carefully smooth it over the pudding. Refrigerate dessert for at least two hours.

Serves 9 to 12

Variation

Add ¼ cup creamy peanut butter to pudding.

Coconut Rice Dessert

2 cups short-grain rice
¼ cup sugar
14 ounces coconut milk
water
additional sugar or brown
    sugar
fresh mango or canned fruit

1. Soak rice in warm water for 20 minutes to soften.

2. Preheat oven to 350°F.

3. Pour coconut milk into a large measuring cup. Add water to make 4½ cups liquid.

4. Pour liquid into a saucepan. Add sugar. Simmer until sugar dissolves.

5. Drain rice. Place rice and liquid in a covered 9 x 13-inch baking dish. Bake for 15 minutes, stir, and bake for an additional 15 to 20 minutes. The liquid will gradually be absorbed by the rice.

6. Serve rice with additional sugar or brown sugar and fruit on top.

Serves 6 to 8

Chewy Chocolate Cookies

1¼ cups butter
2 cups sugar
2 eggs
2 teaspoons vanilla
1 cup brown rice flour
⅔ cup tapioca flour
⅓ cup sorghum flour
1 teaspoon xanthan gum
1 teaspoon soda
¾ teaspoon salt
¾ cup cocoa

1. Preheat oven to 350°F.

2. Mix together butter, sugar, eggs, and vanilla until creamy.

3. Add dry ingredients and mix until combined.

4. Drop by spoonfuls on greased cookie sheet and bake for 9 to 11 minutes.

Makes 44 cookies

Applesauce Cookies

½ cup shortening

1 cup sugar

1 egg

1 teaspoon vanilla

1 cup applesauce

1 cup brown rice flour

½ cup potato starch

½ cup tapioca flour

1 teaspoon baking powder

1½ teaspoons xanthan gum

1 teaspoon baking soda

½ teaspoon salt

½ teaspoon cinnamon

⅛ teaspoon nutmeg

¼ teaspoon cloves

1. Preheat oven to 350°F.

2. Cream shortening, sugar, egg, vanilla, and applesauce. Add dry ingredients and mix thoroughly.

3. Spray cookie sheet with cooking spray. Drop batter by small spoonfuls onto cookie sheet. Bake for 11 to 13 minutes.

Makes 32 cookies

No-Bake Cookies

2 cups sugar

½ cup milk

1 cube butter

5 tablespoons cocoa

3 cups gluten-free oats*
   (be sure these were
   grown separately from
   wheat)

1 teaspoon vanilla

1. Combine sugar, milk, butter, and cocoa. Boil for 1 minute in saucepan.

2. Add oats. Simmer for 5 minutes, stirring constantly, to soften oats. Add vanilla.

3. Using a ¼-cup measuring cup, scoop dollops of mixture onto wax paper. Allow cookies to become firm before eating.

Makes 14 cookies

*Some people with celiac disease cannot tolerate gluten-free oatmeal. Please check with your physician before adding oatmeal to your diet.

Cinnamon Sugar Cookies

½ cup butter, softened

1 cup sugar

1 egg

1 teaspoon vanilla

1⅓ cups brown rice flour

⅔ cup tapioca flour

½ cup sorghum flour

½ teaspoon baking soda

¼ teaspoon salt

1 teaspoon xanthan gum

¼ cup water

3 tablespoons brown sugar

1½ tablespoons cinnamon sugar

1. Cream butter, sugar, egg, and vanilla.
2. Add rice flour, tapioca flour, sorghum flour, baking soda, salt, xanthan gum, and water. Mix thoroughly.
3. Preheat oven to 350°F.
4. Combine brown sugar and cinnamon sugar. Dip spoonful of cookie dough into cinnamon sugar.
5. Place balls of dough on greased cookie sheet. Bake cookies for 11 to 13 minutes.

Makes 24 cookies

Tip: For best results the amount of dough for each cookie should be slightly larger than a whole walnut. Gluten-free cookie dough spreads more than other dough. Let the cookies set for a few minutes before removing them from the cookie sheet.

Sugar Cookies

1 cup sugar
¾ cup butter
1 egg
1 tablespoon sour cream
1 tablespoon vanilla
1 cup brown rice flour
⅓ cup potato starch
⅓ cup tapioca flour
⅛ cup sorghum flour
2 tablespoons corn flour
1 teaspoon baking powder
2 teaspoons xanthan gum

1. Cream together sugar, butter, egg, sour cream, and vanilla.

2. Add dry ingredients and mix just until combined.

3. Divide dough in half and place each section on plastic wrap. Form each section into a log shape. Place dough in fridge for at least 1 hour.

4. Preheat oven to 350°F.

5. Remove dough from fridge and roll again into a log shape, about 1½ inches in diameter. If dough stays in the log shape and is easy to slice, begin cutting dough into ¼-inch slices. If not, return dough to fridge until firm.

6. Spray cookie sheet with cooking spray. Place sliced cookie dough on cookie sheet. Bake for 11 to 13 minutes.

Makes 48 small cookies

Macaroons

11-ounce can sweetened
*   condensed milk*
4 cups flaked coconut
½ cup brown rice flour
⅛ cup tapioca flour

1. Preheat oven to 325°F.

2. Combine condensed milk, coconut, brown rice flour, tapioca flour, egg white, xantham gum, vanilla, and salt in a mixing bowl.

1 egg white
1 teaspoon xantham gum
1 teaspoon vanilla
¼ teaspoon salt

3. Drop dough by the spoonful onto greased cookie sheet. Bake at 325°F for 16 to 18 minutes. Allow to cool, and refrigerate until ready to serve.

Makes 24 to 32 cookies

Chocolate-Chip Cookies

1 cup butter
¾ cup sugar
¾ cup brown sugar
1 teaspoon vanilla
2 eggs
½ cup sorghum flour
2 cups brown rice flour
¾ cup tapioca flour
1 teaspoon xanthan gum
1 teaspoon baking soda
1 teaspoon salt
1½ cups chocolate chips (if milk intolerant, use Enjoy Life R *Chocolate Chips)*

1. Combine butter, sugar, brown sugar, vanilla, and eggs.

2. Add sorghum flour, brown rice flour, tapioca flour, xanthan gum, baking soda, salt, and chocolate chips. Mix thoroughly.

3. Shape into small balls of dough and place on a greased cookie sheet. Bake at 375°F for 10 to 11 minutes.

4. As a variation, substitute ¾ cup butterscotch chips and ⅔ cup toffee bits for chocolate chips.

Makes 36 cookies

Peanut Butter Cookies

1 cup sugar
1 teaspoon baking soda
1 cup creamy peanut butter
1 large egg
½ teaspoon vanilla

1. Preheat oven to 350°F.

2. Mix sugar and baking soda. Add remaining ingredients and mix thoroughly. Chill for 30 minutes in fridge or 10 minutes in freezer.

3. Shape into small balls of dough (about 1 tablespoon each) and place on greased cookie sheet. Bake for 10 minutes.

Makes 27 cookies

Graham Cracker Crust

2 tablespoons brown sugar
⅓ cup sugar
1 cup brown rice flour
⅓ cup tapioca flour
⅛ cup potato starch
⅛ cup sorghum flour
¼ teaspoon salt
½ teaspoon xanthan gum
1 teaspoon baking powder
½ teaspoon baking soda
¼ cup softened butter
2 teaspoons vanilla
2 tablespoons water
¼ cup cooking oil

1. Preheat oven to 325°F.

2. Combine brown sugar, sugar, rice flour, tapioca flour, potato starch, sorghum flour, salt, xanthan gum, baking powder, and baking soda.

3. Add softened butter, vanilla, water, and oil and cut into mixture using pastry blender, two table knives, or a heavy-duty kitchen mixer.

4. Spoon crumbs into pie plate or 9 x 13-inch baking pan and press evenly across the bottom and up the sides. Bake for 20 to 23 minutes for a pie crust or 24 to 26 minutes for a 9 x 13-inch pan.

Makes two small pie crusts or one 9 x 13-inch crust

Pie Crust

½ cup white rice flour or
　　brown rice flour

⅔ cup potato starch

½ cup tapioca flour

3 tablespoons sorghum flour

2 tablespoons masa or corn
　　flour

¾ teaspoon salt

1 teaspoon baking powder

1½ teaspoon xanthan gum

1 tablespoon sugar

¾ cup shortening

1 egg, beaten

½ cup cold water, plus more
　　as needed

1 teaspoon apple cider
　　vinegar

1. Sift rice flour, potato starch, tapioca flour, sorghum flour, corn flour, salt, baking powder, xanthan gum, and sugar into a large mixing bowl.

2. Add shortening and cut it into the dry ingredients with a pastry cutter, two table knives, or a heavy-duty kitchen mixer.

3. In a small bowl, beat egg, water, and vinegar. Add mixture to dry ingredients and mix well. Add more water as needed for a workable (not sticky) texture.

4. Divide the pastry dough into 2 to 3 equal parts, depending on the size of your pie plates. Wrap extra pie crust dough in plastic wrap and place it in a heavy plastic bag in the freezer.

5. Place dough between two sheets of plastic film or parchment paper on kitchen counter and roll out the dough into a pie crust. If pastry dough is sticky and hard to remove from the plastic, pat rice flour over the surface.

6. Remove the top piece of plastic film, then lay the rolled dough in the pie plate. Remove the other piece of plastic film. Flute edges of crust. Prick crust with a fork.

7. For a pre-baked crust, bake at 400°F for 10 to 15 minutes.

Makes 2 to 3 pie crusts

Cream Pie Filling

pie crust
1 cup sugar
¼ cup cornstarch or potato
*   starch*
¼ teaspoon salt
3 cups milk
2 eggs
3 tablespoons butter
1½ teaspoons vanilla
1 baked pie shell
2 sliced bananas or ½ cup
*   shredded coconut*

1. Prepare a gluten-free pie crust or gluten-free graham cracker crust.

2. In a medium saucepan, combine sugar, cornstarch, salt, and milk. Cook and stir over medium heat until thickened and bubbly. Reduce heat, then cook and stir 2 minutes more. Remove from heat.

3. Beat eggs in a small bowl. Remove 1 cup of the hot mixture and allow it to cool slightly. Gradually add it to the eggs two tablespoons at a time. Slowly pour egg mixture into saucepan while stirring. Bring to a gentle boil for 2 minutes, stirring constantly.

4. Remove from heat and add butter and vanilla.

5. Slice bananas and spread across bottom of pie crust. Pour cream filling over bananas. Or add coconut to the cream filling and sprinkle coconut across the top of the pie for a coconut cream pie.

Serves 6 to 8

Apple Pie

1 to 2 quarts gluten-free
*   apple pie filling (see*
*   page 193)*
gluten-free pie crust for
*   bottom and top of pie*

1. Preheat oven to 350°F.

2. Place rolled pie crust dough on pie plate, covering sides and bottom. Allow ¾ inch of extra pie crust around edge.

3. Pour pie filling into uncooked crust. (The amount of pie filling will vary according to the size of the pie plate.) Cover with top pie crust. Fold extra ¾ inch from bottom pie crust over top crust and seal. Flute edge of crust.

4. Cut an apple shape (or slits) into top crust for venting of steam. Bake for 50 to 60 minutes, or until crust is golden brown.

Serves 6 to 8

Peach Pie

2 gluten-free pie crusts
1 cup sugar
1 cup water
3 tablespoons cornstarch
   or potato starch
¼ cup butter
⅛ teaspoon salt
½ teaspoon vanilla or
   almond flavoring
6 to 8 cups fresh peaches

1. Pre-bake two pricked pie crusts at 400°F for 8 to 15 minutes. Allow to cool.

2. Combine sugar, water, cornstarch, butter, and salt in a medium saucepan. Cook and stir until thick and clear. Boil 30 seconds or so. Add vanilla and cool slightly.

3. Slice and peel peaches, then carefully stir into filling mixture. Keep filling separate from pie crust until serving.

Serves 12 to 16

Chocolate Pie

9-inch gluten-free pie
    crust, or gluten-free
    graham cracker crust
one 6-ounce and one
    3.4-ounce box chocolate
    pudding
milk
whipped topping or whipped
    cream

1. Pre-bake pricked crust at 400°F for 8 to 15 minutes (or prepare graham cracker crust.) Allow to cool.

2. Prepare pudding using the amount of milk specified in package instructions. Pour pudding into baked pie crust. Allow to set for several hours.

3. Add whipped topping or whipped cream before serving.

Serves 6 to 8

Pumpkin Pie

2 gluten-free pie crusts
29-ounce can pumpkin
1½ cups sugar
½ teaspoon salt
2 teaspoons cinnamon
1 teaspoon ground ginger
½ teaspoon ground cloves
2 cans evaporated milk, or
    2½ cups almond milk
    or soy milk
4 eggs

1. Preheat oven to 425°F.

2. Place bottom pie crust on pie plate, covering sides and bottom and allowing ½ inch of extra pie crust around edge.

3. Mix pumpkin with remaining ingredients in a large bowl. Pour into uncooked crust. Flute edge of crust.

4. Bake for 15 minutes, then reduce heat to 350°F. Bake for 1 hour if using evaporated milk, or until a knife inserted in center of pie comes out clean. If using almond or soy milk, bake an additional 30 to 40 minutes. Place aluminum foil on outer edge of crust, if needed, to prevent burning.

Serves 6 to 8

Fresh Apple Cake

¾ cup garbanzo or fava
    bean flour
¾ cup brown rice flour
1 cup sugar
½ teaspoon salt
1 teaspoon baking soda
1 teaspoon baking powder
1 teaspoon cinnamon
½ teaspoon nutmeg
1 teaspoon xanthan gum
2 cups coarsely grated
    apples
⅓ cup oil
1 beaten egg
1 teaspoon vanilla
½ cup raisins (optional)
1 cup chopped nuts
    (optional)

Caramel Sauce

1 cube butter
1 cup brown sugar
4 tablespoons milk

1. Preheat oven to 325°F.

2. Combine dry ingredients in large mixing bowl.

3. Combine oil, egg, and vanilla in a small bowl and mix well. Add to the dry ingredients.

4. Add raisins and nuts, if desired. Mix thoroughly.

5. Pour batter in a greased 8 x 8-inch baking pan and bake for 50 to 60 minutes. When done, cake will be brown and spring back if touched in the center.

6. To make caramel sauce, combine ingredients in saucepan and cook over medium heat. Stir until brown sugar is dissolved. Bring to a boil for 1 minute.

7. Pour sauce over hot cake and spread.

Serves 6 to 9

Tip: Prepare different flour combinations in advance and store them in labeled glass jars or sealable plastic bags. It is best to add yeast when mixing the final product.

Poppyseed Cake

3 eggs

1⅛ cups cooking oil

1½ cups milk or soy milk

1½ teaspoons almond
   extract

1½ teaspoons butter-
   flavored extract

1½ teaspoons vanilla

2 cups sugar

2 cups rice flour

1⅛ cups tapioca flour

⅓ cup potato starch

1 tablespoon corn flour

2½ tablespoons sorghum
   flour

1 teaspoon salt

1½ teaspoons baking
   powder

1 teaspoon xanthan gum

1 tablespoon poppyseeds

Glaze

¼ cup undiluted limeade or
   orange juice concentrate

¾ cup powdered sugar

½ teaspoon almond extract

½ teaspoon butter-flavored
   extract

½ teaspoon vanilla

1. Preheat oven to 350°F.

2. Blend eggs, oil, milk, almond extract, butter-flavored extract, and vanilla in a mixing bowl.

3. Add dry ingredients and mix until combined. To remove some of the lumps that remain, press the batter with a rubber spatula.

4. Pour batter into a greased 9 x 13-inch baking pan. Bake for 40 to 45 minutes, or until a toothpick insterted in the center of the cake comes out clean.

5. To make glaze, bring juice concentrate and powdered sugar to a boil for 1 minute. Remove from heat and add extracts and vanilla.

6. Poke holes in warm cake with a toothpick and drizzle glaze over cake.

Serves 9 to 12

Carrot Cake

*¾ cup garbanzo or fava bean
    flour*
¾ cup rice flour
¼ cup potato flour
¼ cup tapioca flour
2 teaspoons xanthan gum
1 teaspoon baking powder
2 teaspoons baking soda
½ teaspoon salt
1½ cups cooking oil
4 eggs
2 cups sugar
2 cups finely grated carrots
*8-ounce can crushed
    pineapple, drained*

Nuts (Optional)

*1 cup chopped pecans or
    almonds*
3 tablespoons honey
2 teaspoons cinnamon
¼ teaspoon nutmeg
1 tablespoon butter

1. Preheat oven to 375°F.

2. Mix dry ingredients in a large mixing bowl.

3. Beat oil, eggs, sugar, grated carrots, and crushed pineapple for three minutes in another bowl.

4. Add egg mixture to flour mixture and mix until combined.

5. If you wish to add nuts, place the chopped nuts in a small, nonstick frying pan and add honey, cinnamon, nutmeg, and butter. Heat until warm, then add to cake batter.

6. Pour batter into a greased 9 x 13-inch glass baking pan and bake for 60 to 65 minutes. Cool before frosting with Cream Cheese Frosting (see page 174).

Serves 9 to 12

Cream Cheese Frosting

4-ounce package cream
    cheese, softened
¼ cup butter
1 teaspoon vanilla
½ teaspoon grated lemon
    zest (optional)
1 teaspoon lemon juice
1½ cups powdered sugar

1. Cream together cream cheese, butter, and vanilla.
2. Add lemon zest (optional), lemon juice, and powdered sugar. Mix until smooth. Frost carrot cake when cool.

Fantastic Cake

gluten-free yellow or white
    cake mix that makes two
    9-inch-round cakes
20-ounce can crushed
    pineapple, undrained
11-ounce can mandarin
    oranges, undrained
2 eggs
¼ cup cooking oil
4-ounce package cream
    cheese, softened
8-ounce container whipped
    topping

1. Drain ½ cup crushed pineapple to use in topping. (This will yield about ⅓ cup crushed pineapple.)
2. Using an electric mixer, beat cake mix, 1 cup undrained pineapple, mandarin oranges with juice (reserve 6 orange segments), eggs, and oil on medium speed for about one minute. Bake at 350°F for 28 to 35 minutes.
3. To make topping, place reserved orange segments, reserved drained pineapple, and cream cheese in a mixing bowl and beat well. Fold in whipped topping.
4. Spread topping over cooled cake prior to serving.

Serves 10 to 12

Moist Chocolate Cake

¾ cup brown rice flour

1⅔ cup tapioca flour

⅓ cup potato starch

⅓ cup sorghum flour

2¾ cups sugar

3 tablespoons Dutch cocoa

1 tablespoon baking soda

1 teaspoon salt

1½ teaspoons xanthan gum

3 tablespoons apple cider vinegar

¾ cup cooking oil

2⅔ cups water

1 tablespoon vanilla

Chocolate Frosting

1 cube butter

4 teaspoons Dutch cocoa

¼ cup milk

2 cups miniature marshmallows

1 teaspoon vanilla

2 cups powdered sugar

1. Preheat oven to 375°F.

2. To make the cake, mix brown rice flour, tapioca flour, potato starch, sorghum flour, sugar, cocoa, baking soda, salt, and xanthan gum in a large mixing bowl.

3. Add vinegar, oil, water, and vanilla and mix thoroughly.

4. Spray a 9 x 13-inch baking pan with cooking spray. Pour batter into pan. Bake for 40 to 45 minutes.

5. To make the frosting, bring butter, cocoa, and milk to a boil. Add marshmallows, vanilla, and powdered sugar. Mix with whisk and frost cake while cake is still warm.

Serves 8 to 12

Angel Food Cake

1½ cups powdered sugar
½ cup brown rice flour
¼ cup potato starch
1 teaspoon xanthan gum
¼ cup tapioca flour
1½ cups egg whites (about
    12 egg whites)
1½ teaspoons cream of
    tartar
1 cup sugar
1½ teaspoons vanilla
½ teaspoon almond extract
¼ teaspoon salt
strawberries
heavy whipping cream
3 tablespoons powdered
    sugar

1. Heat oven to 375°F. Mix powdered sugar (do not use granulated sugar), rice flour, potato starch, xanthan gum, and tapioca flour in a plastic storage bag or mixing bowl. Set aside.

2. Beat egg whites and cream of tartar in a separate 3-quart bowl on medium speed until foamy. Beat in sugar on high speed, ⅛ cup at a time, adding vanilla, almond extract, and salt with the last addition of sugar. Continue beating until stiff and glossy. Do not underbeat.

3. Sprinkle powdered sugar–flour mixture, ¼ cup at a time, over meringue, folding in with a rubber spatula until powdered sugar–flour mixture disappears. Spread batter into an ungreased angel-food cake pan. Cut gently through batter with knife.

4. Bake until cracks on top of cake feel dry and the top springs back when touched lightly, about 30 to 35 minutes. Invert pan on heatproof funnel (or a can of unopened food) until cool. Wash and slice strawberries.

5. Whip the cream and add 3 tablespoons powdered sugar. Combine strawberries and whipped cream. Serve over cake.

Serves 6 to 8

Tip: If you don't have an angel-food cake pan, you can use two 8-inch or two 9-inch round cake pans. Coat each pan with shortening or cooking spray and line the pan with a round piece of waxed paper, sprayed lightly with cooking spray. Bake cakes at 350°F for 35 to 40 minutes or until cake pulls away from the sides of the pan, and the center springs back when touched.

Fluffy Frosting

4 cups powdered sugar
¼ cup water
¾ cup shortening
½ teaspoon almond flavoring
½ teaspoon butter flavoring
½ teaspoon vanilla
pink food coloring (optional)

Whip ingredients with hand mixer until well mixed.

Cake Decorating Frosting

2½ cups powdered sugar
¼ cup shortening
⅛ cup butter, softened
2 teaspoons egg white
¼ teaspoon salt
¼ teaspoon vanilla
¼ teaspoon lemon flavoring
1 teaspoon almond flavoring
2½ tablespoons milk

Combine all ingredients and whip with hand mixer for 4 to 5 minutes on medium speed.

Strawberry Cheesecake

graham cracker crust (see
    page 166)
8-ounce package cream
    cheese
1½ cups powdered sugar
1 cup heavy whipping cream
4.75-ounce box strawberry
    Junket* Danish Dessert
10 to 15 strawberries, sliced

1. Prepare graham cracker crust and press into bottom of a 9 x 13-inch casserole dish.

2. Cream together cream cheese and powdered sugar.

3. Whip cream in a separate bowl until stiff peaks form. Fold whipped cream into mixture of cream cheese and powdered sugar.

4. Drop by small spoonfuls onto crust and spread carefully. Place in fridge.

5. In a saucepan with tall sides, prepare Danish Dessert according to package directions.

6. Allow to cool slightly, then add strawberries. Pour over cream cheese layer. Cover and allow to set up in fridge for 4 to 5 hours.

Serves 9 to 12

Blueberry Baked Cheesecake

graham cracker crust (see
    page 166)
five 8-ounce packages
    cream cheese
1¾ cups sugar
3 tablespoons brown rice
    flour

1. Press crust into bottom and sides of a 9-inch springform pan and bake as directed on page 166.

2. Beat cream cheese in large bowl for 30 seconds. Add sugar, brown rice flour, lemon zest, and vanilla and beat until smooth.

3. Add eggs and egg yolks one at a time and mix. On low speed, add cream.

½ *teaspoon grated lemon zest*

2 *teaspoons vanilla*

5 *eggs*

2 *egg yolks*

½ *cup heavy whipping cream*

blueberry pie filling

4. Scoop filling into baked crust and bake at 500°F for 12 minutes, then 200°F for 1 hour. Leave in oven for 30 min. with door ajar.

5. Refrigerate for 6 hours. Top with blueberry pie filling.

Delicious Waffle Cones

1 *egg*

1 *egg white*

¼ *teaspoon salt*

⅓ *cup sugar*

¾ *to 1 cup Pamela's*™

    Baking and Pancake Mix

2 *tablespoons melted butter*

This recipe is for use with The Original Waffle Cone Maker.®

1. Preheat the waffle cone maker.

2. Place the egg, egg white, salt, and sugar in a small mixing bowl. Mix well with a whisk for about one minute.

3. Whisk in the gluten-free baking mix until there are no lumps. Add the melted butter and mix well.

4. Pour 2 to 3 tablespoons of batter into waffle iron. Cook for 40 to 50 seconds. Remove cone from waffle iron with a heat-proof spatula. Shape into cone, according to waffle cone maker directions.

Serves 5 to 7

Brownies

4 eggs, beaten
2 cups sugar
5 tablespoons Dutch cocoa
2 teaspoons vanilla
¾ cup rice flour
½ cup tapioca flour
¼ cup potato starch
⅛ cup sorghum flour
⅛ cup corn flour
2 teaspoons xanthan gum
1 teaspoon baking powder
½ pound melted butter
½ cup mint baking chips
    (optional)

Hot Fudge Icing

¼ cup butter
1 cup sugar
¼ cup milk
⅔ cup milk chocolate chips
¾ cup miniature
    marshmallows
1 teaspoon vanilla
½ cup mint baking chips
    (optional)*

1. Preheat oven to 350°F.

2. Beat eggs. Add sugar and mix well.

3. Mix in remaining ingredients except melted butter. Batter will be thick. Gradually add melted butter.

4. Bake for 35 to 38 minutes in a greased 9 x 13-inch baking pan. For a crispier brownie, bake on a greased jelly-roll pan covered with parchment paper and reduce baking time to 20 to 25 minutes.

5. To make Hot Fudge Icing, melt butter in saucepan. Add sugar and milk. Boil for one minute. Remove from heat and add chocolate chips, marshmallows, and vanilla. Stir until well mixed. Let the frosting cool before spreading on brownies or frosting will be runny.

6. If adding mint baking chips, do not add them to frosting mixture. Melt mint baking chips in microwave and drizzle across frosted brownies.

Serves 9 to 12

Drinks
and
Miscellaneous

Refreshing Berry Punch

12-ounce can frozen white
    grape juice
2 liters grapefruit soda
1 cup frozen berry medley of
    choice
ice

In large punch bowl, reconstitute juice by adding water. Stir in grapefruit soda. Add fruit and ice.

Serves 10 to 12

Homemade Root Beer

5 pounds sugar
5 gallons water
2-ounce bottle root beer
    concentrate
5-pound block of dry ice

Combine first three ingredients in large 10-gallon insulated drink cooler container. Using clean gloves, add dry ice to mixture.

Serves a large group

Grape Juice Lemonade

12-ounce can frozen
    grape juice concentrate
12-ounce can frozen
    lemonade concentrate
water
3 cans lemon-lime soda
½ cup sugar

In large insulated drink cooler container, add water to grape juice and lemonade concentrates according to directions on cans and mix them together. Add soda pop and sugar and mix well.

Serves 12 to 14

Orange Juice Refresher

*6-ounce can frozen orange
    juice concentrate*
2 cups milk
½ cup sugar
1 teaspoon vanilla
¼ cup powdered milk
12 ice cubes

Combine all ingredients in blender until smooth.

Serves 5 to 7

Tip: For a delicious variation, replace the orange juice with other juice, such as white grape juice, raspberry lemonade, fruit medley, etc.

Delicious Slush

*12-ounce can strawberry
    guava juice concentrate*
water
1-liter bottle Fresca®

1. Prepare juice in a large pitcher according to instructions on can. Freeze juice.
2. Pour soda over juice. As it softens, break up frozen juice.
3. Pour mixture into large punch bowl for serving, if desired.

Serves 8 to 10

Peanut Butter Play Dough

1 cup creamy peanut butter
1¼ cups dry milk
1 cup light corn syrup
1¼ cups powdered sugar

Place all ingredients in a sealed bag. Knead until a dough forms.

Rice-Flour Play Dough

2¼ cups rice flour
1¾ cups salt
1 tablespoon cream of tartar
2½ tablespoons cooking oil
2 cups colored water

1. Heat over medium heat until thickened.

2. Remove from heat, and then knead. If play dough is too sticky, add more rice flour.

Toasted Pumpkin Seeds

1 cup pumpkin seeds
1 tablespoon cooking oil or
*   melted butter*
salt

1. Preheat oven to 350°F. Wash pumpkin seeds and dry them on a paper towel.

2. Place pumpkin seeds in a plastic bag or bowl. Mix seeds with cooking oil or melted butter. Spread seeds on baking sheet and sprinkle with salt. Bake for 15 to 20 minutes, stirring several times.

Tip: For a 72-hour emergency kit, consider storing sunflower and pumpkin seeds, almonds, fruit snacks, gluten-free jerky, tuna, water, and dehydrated mashed potatoes.

Tip: Surprise your family and tell them you are pretending there is an emergency. Take your 72-hour kit to a nearby park and test it out. Rotate food that may have expired.

Canning

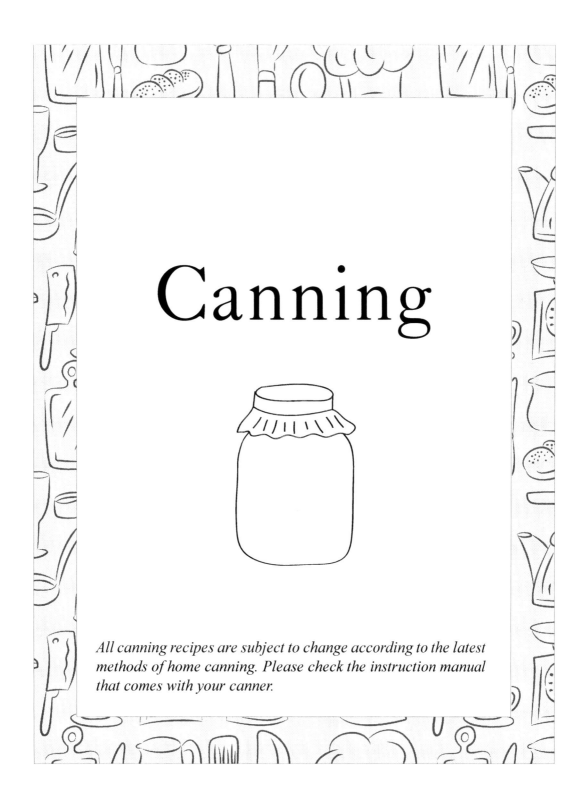

All canning recipes are subject to change according to the latest methods of home canning. Please check the instruction manual that comes with your canner.

Salsa

5 quarts tomatoes, peeled
    and quartered
3 red or green bell peppers,
    diced
3 yellow bell peppers, diced
2½ jalapeno peppers
    (remove some seeds for
    milder salsa), diced
2 Anaheim peppers (long,
    green variety), diced
2 long red peppers, diced
2 large onions, diced
3 cloves garlic, minced
1½ teaspoons paprika
⅓ cup sugar
½ cup apple cider vinegar
1½ teaspoons coarse ground
    pepper
¼ cup canning salt
1½ teaspoons cumin
1½ teaspoons garlic salt
½ bunch cilantro, chopped
1 quart tomato paste
    (optional)

1. Cook tomatoes, peppers, onions, and garlic in large pot until tender (about 1 hour). Stir occasionally.

2. Add paprika, sugar, vinegar, coarse ground pepper, canning salt, cumin, garlic salt, cilantro, and tomato paste, if desired. Simmer for 1 hour, stirring occasionally.

3. Wash quart or pints jars and fill with salsa to ½ inch from top.

4. Simmer lids and keep in hot water for at least 3 to 4 minutes. Place lids and canning rings on jars and tighten.

5. Place filled jars in the canner and cover completely with water. Turn heat to high and begin timing when the water is boiling. Make sure a softly rolling boil is maintained. Turn heat down to medium high and process 25 minutes in a boiling water bath.

Makes 8 to 14 pints or 4 to 7 quarts

Tip: Peppers and onions can be diced quickly by placing them, in batches, in a blender, covering them with water, and then pulsing blender. Drain off extra water before adding peppers and onions to pot.

Dill Pickles

cucumbers to fill 7 jars
12 cups water
6 cups apple cider vinegar
¾ cup canning or non-
    iodized salt
7 heads of fresh dill
14 garlic cloves

1. Wash 7 quart jars. Wash cucumbers and soak in ice water for 24 hours. Drain cucumbers.

2. Place 1 head of dill and 2 garlic cloves in the bottom of each quart jar. Boil water, vinegar, and salt for one minute. (Less brine may be needed, depending on whether slices or whole pickles are desired.)

3. Place cucumbers in jars. Pour water, vinegar, and salt mixture over cucumbers and fill the quart jars to ½ inch from top.

4. Simmer lids and keep in hot water for 3 to 4 minutes. Place lids and canning rings on jars and tighten.

5. Bring water to nearly a boil in canner. Do not allow brine in jars to cool, or the jars may break when you add them to the hot water in the canner. Add quarts of pickles to hot water using a bottle lifter. Use caution to avoid getting burned by the hot water. Process in a boiling water bath for 15 minutes.

6. Wait 2 to 3 weeks before eating pickles.

Makes 7 quarts

Dill Beans

green beans, with ends
   removed
1 garlic clove per jar
1 dill weed sprig per jar
¼ teaspoon alum per jar
2 cups water
1 cup white vinegar
2 tablespoons non-iodized
   salt

1. In each quart jar, place one garlic clove, a sprig of dill weed, and ¼ teaspoon alum. Line jar with beans. Calculate amount of brine to prepare depending on amount of beans. Bring brine to a boil and pour over beans to ½ inch from top of jar.

2. Simmer lids and keep in hot water for 3 to 4 minutes. Place lids and canning rings on jars and tighten.

3. Place the filled jars in the canner and cover completely with water. Turn heat to high and begin timing when the water is boiling. Make sure a softly rolling boil is maintained. Turn heat down to medium high and process 7 minutes in a boiling water bath.

Green Beans

green beans
1 teaspoon salt per quart
boiling water

Due to the dangers of using a pressure canner, do not use this recipe without a thorough knowledge of the process of pressure canning. Read the manual that came with your pressure canner. The boiling water bath method is not a safe way to can beans.

1. Remove ends of beans. Snap and wash beans.

2. Put 1 teaspoon salt in a quart jar. Fill quart jar with green beans, allowing 1 inch space at top

of jar. Add boiling water to 1 inch from top.

3. Simmer lids and keep in hot water for 3 to 4 minutes. Place lids and canning rings on jars and tighten.

4. Place jars in pressure canner with 2 quarts of hot water (check pressure canner instructions to verify water amount). Lock pressure canner lid. Turn heat on high, and when pressure builds in canner (approximately 15 to 20 minutes) to 15 pounds pressure (for quarts), begin timing. It is important to check canner pressure often to make sure it stays at 15 pounds pressure. Turn heat down to medium high and process for 25 minutes. Process 20 minutes for pints. Certain types of pressure canners can be tested by a hardware store or county agent to ensure the pressure reading is correct.

Frozen Corn

30 cups raw corn (cut from cob)
12 cups water
1 cup sugar
¼ cup salt

1. Combine corn with water, sugar, and salt in a very large pot or canner. Simmer for 20 minutes.

2. When cool enough, place in fridge. Or place a block of ice or some ice cubes (in a clean plastic bag) in hot corn to cool it quickly. Place corn in ziptop freezer bags and freeze.

Tip: Here is a quick method for removing corn from the cobs: place each cob of corn on hole of angel food cake pan. Using an electric knife, carefully slice corn off cob into cake pan, rotating cob as you go.

Tomato Juice

6 quarts tomatoes
2 cups onions (in quarters)
2 cups celery
6 bay leaves
salt, to taste

1. Wash 5 quart jars. Cook ingredients together until tender.

2. Remove bay leaves. Pour mixture through food mill. Add salt, to taste.

3. Fill the quart jars to ½ inch from top with tomato juice.

4. Simmer lids and keep in hot water for 3 to 4 minutes. Place lids and canning rings on jars and tighten.

5. Place the filled jars in the canner and cover completely with water. Turn heat to high and begin timing when the water is boiling. Make sure a softly rolling boil is maintained. Turn heat down to medium high and process 10 minutes in boiling water bath.

Makes 5 quarts

Grape Juice

Concord grapes
½ cup sugar per quart jar
boiling water

1. Fill clean sink about halfway with cold water and add Concord grapes. Remove good grapes from stems and rinse under cold water.

2. Fill each quart jar about halfway with grapes. Add ½ cup sugar, then fill to ½-inch head space with boiling water.

3. Simmer lids and allow to stay in hot water for at least 3 to 4 minutes. Place lids and canning rings on jars and tighten.

4. Place the filled jars in the canner and cover completely with water. Turn heat to high and begin timing when the water is boiling. Turn heat down to medium high and process 15 minutes in boiling water bath. Make sure a softly rolling boil is maintained.

5. Wait until sugar dissolves in the bottom of the jars before using grape juice. Remove grapes from juice before serving juice.

Pears

ripe pears
½ cup sugar per quart
boiling water

1. Use carrot peeler to remove skin from pears. Cut pear in half and remove seeds with small metal measuring spoon. Wash pears well and fill quart jar, allowing a 1-inch space at top of jar. Pour ½ cup sugar over fruit in jar. Add boiling water to ½-inch head space.

2. Simmer lids and keep in hot water for 3 to 4 minutes. Place lids and canning rings on jars and tighten.

3. Place the filled jars in the canner and cover completely with water. Turn heat to high and begin timing when the water is boiling. Make sure a softly rolling boil is maintained. Turn heat down to medium high and process 20 minutes in boiling water bath.

Peaches

ripened peaches
½ cup sugar per quart
boiling water

1. Blanch peaches by submerging them in boiling water for about 15 seconds. Place them in a clean sink filled halfway with cold water.

2. Cut peaches in half and remove skin and pit.

3. Wash quart jars and fill with peaches, allowing a 1-inch space at top of each jar. Pour ½ cup sugar over fruit in each jar. Add boiling water to ½-inch head space.

4. Simmer lids and keep in hot water for 3 to 4 minutes. Place lids and canning rings on jars and tighten.

5. Place the filled jars in the canner and cover completely with water. Turn heat to high and begin timing when the water is boiling. Make sure a softly rolling boil is maintained. Turn heat down to medium high and process 20 minutes in boiling water bath.

Raspberries

9 cups raspberries
2 cups sugar
5 cups water

1. Wash 5 to 6 pint jars. Fill clean sink with water and add raspberries. Let them soak for several minutes and lightly rinse them under a gentle stream of water. Try not to handle them too much.

2. Fill jars ⅔ full with raspberries. Bring water and sugar to a boil until sugar dissolves. Fill to ½-inch head space with water–sugar solution.

3. Simmer lids and keep in hot water for 3 to 4 minutes. Place lids and canning rings on jars and tighten.

4. Place the filled jars in the canner and cover completely with water. Turn heat to high and begin timing when the water is boiling. Make sure a softly rolling boil is maintained. Turn heat down to medium high and process 10 minutes in boiling water bath.

Apple Pie Filling

12 quarts peeled, cored, and
*   sliced McIntosh apples*
5 quarts water
5 cups sugar
1 teaspoon nutmeg
1 cup cornstarch
1 tablespoon cinnamon
1 teaspoon salt
2 tablespoons lemon juice

1. Wash 8 quart jars. Place apples in a large pot with water. Cook for 10 minutes to shrink apples. Remove apples with a slotted spoon.

2. Add remaining ingredients to juice from apples. Cook until thickened and add apples. Fill the quart jars to ½ inch from top.

3. Simmer lids and keep in hot water for 3 to 4 minutes. Place lids and canning rings on jars and tighten.

4. Place the filled jars in the canner and cover completely with water. Turn heat to high and begin timing when the water is boiling. Make sure a softly rolling boil is maintained. Turn heat down to medium high and process 20 minutes in boiling water bath.

Makes 8 quarts

Applesauce

Apples, peeled, cored, and
    sliced (an average
    of 19 pounds is needed
    per canner load of 7
    quarts, or 12 to 14
    pounds for 9 pints)
¼ cup sugar per pound of
    apples, to taste
⅛ teaspoon salt per pound
    of apples, to taste

1. Wash apples, cut them into quarters, then peel and core them. Place in heavy 8- to 10-quart pan for a canner batch of applesauce. Add ¾ cup of water (if using 19 pounds of apples) and heat the apples over medium heat, stirring often to move apple slices from bottom to top. Heat until apples are tender.

2. Pour apples into a food strainer–sauce maker. Pureé, then add sugar and salt. Pour hot applesauce into clean jars to ½ inch from the top.

3. Simmer lids and keep in hot water for 3 to 4 minutes. Place lids and canning rings on jars and tighten.

4. Place the filled jars in the canner and cover completely with water. Turn heat to high and begin timing when the water is boiling. Make sure a softly rolling boil is maintained. Turn heat down to medium high and process 20 minutes in boiling water bath.

Resources

Websites

www.celiac.com (for information about celiac disease),

www.enterolab.com (a possible way to test for celiac disease),

www.mayoclinic.com (good summary of what celiac disease is)

www.celiacdiseasecenter.columbia.edu/ (excellent source for information)

www.celiacchicks.com

www.celiaccenter.org

www.glutenfree.com

www.livingwithout.com

www.wheatlessandmeatless.com

www.blog.fatfreevegan.com

www.glutenfreeforgood.com/blog/

www.simplerecipes.com/recipes/gluten-free

www.123glutenfree.com

Organizations

CSA:http://www.csaceliacs.org/

GIG:http://www.gfco.org/

Labeling Standards: http://www.fda.gov/Food/LabelingNutrition/FoodLabeling
GuidanceRegulatoryInformation/Topic-SpecificLabelingInformation/default.htm

Index by Recipe Name

Biography

For many years, Susan Bell suffered from stomach problems, but she thought it was just part of life. In 2003, her sister found out that their mother's celiac disease was genetic, and the mystery of health issues began to be solved with a diagnosis of celiac disease for Susan, her sister, and several other siblings. When Susan got tired of living on tortilla chips, she began converting her favorite recipes into gluten-free recipes. She found that with a great cookbook and a menu plan, family mealtime could be a happy experience, and that her attitude made all the difference in how her children handled their own celiac disease. She and her sister started a support group to help others cope with the disease.

Susan enjoys learning from others and can be contacted at gfcookingmadeeasy@gmail.com. Please visit her blog at www.gluten-freecookingmadeeasy.blogspot.com.